Wild, Wild World of Animals

The Cats

A TIME-LIFE TELEVISION BOOK

Produced in Association with Vineyard Books, Inc.

Editor: Eleanor Graves
Project Director: Albert R. Leventhal
Senior Editor: Lucille Ogle
Text Editor: Richard Oulahan
    Associate Text Editor: Bonnie Johnson
    Advisory Editor: Bertel Bruun
    Contributing Authors: Maitland A. Edey, Lesley Bayes, Roger Caras,
        Thomas A. Dozier, John Gooders, Paul Trachtman
    Assistant Editor: Regina Grant Hersey
    Research: Jo-Anne Cienski, Ellen Schachter, Elsie Washington
    Copy Editor: Robert J. Myer
Picture Editor: Richard O. Pollard
    Picture Research: Barbara Crosby, Judith Greene
Book Designer and Art Director: Jos. Trautwein
Production Coordinator: Jane Quinson

WILD, WILD WORLD OF ANIMALS

TELEVISION PROGRAM

Producers: Jonathan Donald and Lothar Wolff

This Time-Life Television book is published by Time-Life Films, Inc.

Bruce L. Paisner, *President*

J. Nicoll Durrie, *Vice President*

Wild, Wild World of Animals

The Cats

Based on the television series
Wild, Wild World of Animals

Published by
TIME-LIFE FILMS

The introduction by Maitland A. Edey was adapted from *The Cats of Africa*, a Time-Life Book © 1968 Time Inc.

Excerpt reprinted by permission of Charles Scribner's Sons from "The Short Happy Life of Francis Macomber" by Ernest Hemingway from The Short Stories of Ernest Hemingway. *Story copyright 1936 Ernest Hemingway. Reprinted also by permission of Jonathan Cape Ltd., publishers, with acknowledgment to the Executors of the Ernest Hemingway Estate.*

"The Tyger" reprinted from Songs of Innocence and of Experience *by William Blake, 1826 edition, by permission of the United States Library of Congress, Rosenwald Collection.*

Excerpt from African Genesis *by Robert Ardrey, copyright © 1961 by Literat S. A. Reprinted by permission of Atheneum Publishers, New York, and Wm. Collins Sons & Co., Ltd., United Kingdom.*

Excerpt from Lions, Gorillas and Their Neighbors *by Carl Akeley, published by Stanley Paul in 1931, reprinted by permission of Hutchinson Publishing Group Ltd.*

"Mountain Lion" from The Complete Poems of D. H. Lawrence, *edited by Vivian de Sola Pinto and F. Warren Roberts. Copyright © 1964, 1971 by Angelo Ravagli and C. M. Weekley, Executors of the Estate of Frieda Lawrence Ravagli. All rights reserved. Reprinted by permission of The Viking Press, Inc. with acknowledgment to William Heinemann Ltd., publishers, Laurence Pollinger Ltd., author's agent, and the Estate of Mrs. Frieda Lawrence.*

Contents

Introduction *by Maitland A. Edey*

IN THINKING ABOUT the how and the why of cats, the first question one is likely to stumble over is: Where did they come from, for not so very long ago there were no cats anywhere on earth. Like all other existing animals, they have evolved from older forms. And while it might be interesting to trace feline ancestry back half a billion years or so to the origins of life, it is more useful to go back a mere 190 million years and look at a group of small, long-extinct, insect-eating, warm-blooded creatures that were the ancestors of all mammals: men, horses, porcupines, mice—and cats.

It was not until about 60 million years ago that the descendants of those original insectivores had branched out into a variety of types—or evolutionary lines—that began to resemble animals we might recognize today.

One such line starts with a small group that had graduated from insect-eating to meat-eating. These were the miacids, the ancestors of all living carnivores. Like their insect-eating forebears, they were generally small, long-bodied, short-legged, and had long, narrow snouts. But their skulls were larger, and it is believed that their brains were considerably more complex.

By about 20 million years ago the miacids, in turn, had evolved into other things, specifically into the ten presently known families of meat-eaters. Three of those families—the seals, sea lions, and walruses—moved back to the sea (where all living creatures originated), undergoing drastic changes in their physical equipment. Of the seven families that stayed on land—the raccoons, bears, dogs, weasels, genets, hyenas, and cats—none took the bizarre forms of their seagoing cousins. There was no need to. The original miacids were general utility-model carnivores, and their land-based descendants simply improved on the original model. They became swifter, keener-eyed, and more acute in nose and ear—but otherwise not too different. Cats make this point neatly. To bring down a zebra requires a large predator, such as a lion; a smaller predator, for example a house cat, will naturally attack smaller prey, such as a mouse; but the basic animal is essentially the same. Nevertheless, there are differences among carnivores. Some, like dogs, rely on a keen sense of smell. Cats depend more on sight and hearing and, surprisingly, on touch, which accounts for their magnificent whiskers. Cats do much of their hunting at night, and whiskers enable them to move through dense cover, feeling their way as they go, aware of twigs and leaves, which they are able to touch with their whiskers without disturbing them.

All carnivores have large, well-developed canines and incisors for fighting, killing, and tearing hunks of meat from a carcass. Other teeth, called carnassials, have a shearing effect when lower jaw meets upper. It is in the molars farther back in the jaw that wolves and other meat-eaters are better endowed. Somewhere during evolution the cat's ancestors lost some of these teeth, which is not surprising, because a molar is for grinding, and a cat does not grind its food. Cats chew scarcely at all. As soon as they succeed in getting a manageable piece of meat into the mouth they swallow it. They are unable to

8

THE EVOLUTION OF THE CATS

The three branches of the modern cat family—Small Cats, Big Cats, and the distinctive Cheetah—began to evolve from their common ancestors, the Neofelids, about 40 million years ago. About the same time a secondary branch of felines, the Paleofelids, appeared, represented by two groups, the Nimravines and the Ancient Saber-toothed Cats. These flourished for about 30 million years until, for unknown reasons, the line became extinct. The Neofelids, however, continued to evolve and about 20 million years ago produced Pseudaelurus, whose descendants included another saber-toothed family of which Smilodon was the largest and the last, dying out about 10,000 years ago. From the Neofelids also came a group of primitive animals, such as Dinofelis, which, for about five million years, were the only large-bodied cats in existence. They were the same size as the lions, and they disappeared about one million years ago just as today's cats first appeared.

Cheetah   Big Cats   Small Cats

Today

Saber-toothed Cats

Smilodon

1 million years ago

Primitive Big Cats
Dinofelis

10 million years ago

Nimravines

Ancient Saber-toothed Cats

Nimravus

Eusmilus

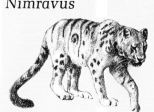

20 million years ago

Pseudaelurus

30 million years ago

NEOFELIDS   PALEOFELIDS

40 million years ago

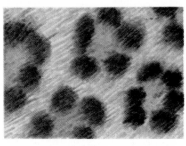

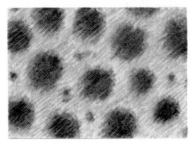

To the inexperienced cat-watcher, the spots on the coats of the jaguar, leopard, and cheetah may appear exactly alike. The drawings above, however, illustrate the distinct variations among them. The jaguar's spots (top) are clumped together, usually in groups of four or five, to form rosettes that surround one or more dark spots. The leopard's fur (center) is also decorated with rosette shapes but with unspotted centers that are a shade darker than the cat's yellowish overall background hair. The cheetah's fur has distinct black spots (bottom) that form no other pattern.

grind up large bones. A cat's jaw works only in two directions: up and down. To grind large bones, one must also be able to move the jaw sideways, as dogs—and humans—do.

Because a cat has fewer teeth than a dog, its muzzle is shorter, its face flatter. Another reason for this facial configuration is that a cat depends on its eyes more than a dog does. However, both are hunting animals and must be able to judge distances of moving prey precisely. Therefore, their eyes face forward rather than to the side. This means that the field of view of each eye overlaps that of the other, providing what is known as binocular vision and thus giving extremely good depth perception. Herbivores do not need binocular vision; their food is standing still. What they do need is to be able to see potential enemies coming from any direction. Consequently their eyes are on the sides of their heads. A rabbit can see forward, upward, backward, and sideward, but in each of these directions with only one eye. What the world looks like to a rabbit is impossible for humans to imagine because we have binocular vision like cats. Thus it is probable that we see things pretty much as cats do—although they are believed to be color-blind, and also we can never be sure quite how they see things because their brains are constructed differently.

A cat's eyes are placed right in front, wide and unblinking, on each side of the nose, like an owl's. Cats never look out of the corners of their eyes at things. They swivel their heads and stare directly at them. A dog, by contrast, will lie on the floor, its chin outstretched, and if it wants to look at something it will often roll its eyes upward without moving its head at all.

Cat's eyes are splendid instruments. They can apparently focus clearly at any distance. One need only observe a cat intently watching a fly as it buzzes around a room to realize how well its vision accommodates. The speed and small size of the fly, and its quick changes of position from near to far, are difficult for the human eye to focus on and follow, but they do not bother a cat. A man will lose sight of the fly repeatedly, and it is only when it shows up momentarily against a windowpane or a white wall that the human eye can pick it up again. A cat can keep its eye on any fly with ease.

Another special piece of equipment peculiar to a cat is its tongue. This is covered with small projections called papillae, which resemble the points on a wood rasp. Among house cats the papillae are small and give only a slightly rough feeling when one's hand is licked. But among the larger cats the papillae are formidable instruments. A few swipes from a lion's tongue could take the skin right off the back of a human hand. Although it is primarily a body-cleaning tool, the tongue is also an important part of the feeding equipment. A pride of hungry lions will polish off a freshly killed zebra in half an hour. All the bones will be licked clean, except those of the lower legs.

A cat's body is long and supple. Its bones, though not particularly large for the size of the animal, get their strength from the density of their material. Complementing these moderately sized but strong bones is a set of equally strong muscles and sinews on which the bones are rather loosely strung together. It is this loose structure that gives a cat its surpassing grace and sinuosity of movement.

The legs of most cats are moderate in length and again characterized by great strength. Not only do they provide sudden power for springing on prey, but they also serve well in fighting, tipped as they are with the sharpest claws of all carnivores (the long-legged, dull-clawed cheetah is an exception). These claws are under the control of their owner and ordinarily are kept sheathed.

In overall body proportions the cats are remarkably alike, although there are a few obvious variations. The cheetah is atypical in seeming to have legs that are too long and a head that is too small. The male lion seems to have too large a head and the serval ears designed for a cat one size larger. All cats have long tails except for the lynx and bobcat and a few domestic varieties such as the Manx cat. Where the lynx, bobcat, and Manx tails went—and why—no one knows, for tails are certainly among the most expressive of a cat's appurtenances. They curl and coil snugly in sleep. They loop and droop in ineffable indolence from leopards drowsing in trees. They switch back and forth with hair-raising tension in a cat about to spring. They stand straight as masts in a confident kitchen-strolling tabby.

The coats of cats vary in color, although the great majority of them tend to be tawny in tone—presumably for concealment. Spots, polka dots, rosettes, and stripes abound. Even lions, which appear to be of a uniform sandy hue, are spotted when young, and many of them carry faint spots on their flanks and legs well up into maturity. Every living species of cat has one marking in common, the tear stripe at the inner corner of each eye.

The coat, or fur, that bears all these markings also varies. As a general rule, the larger the species the coarser the hairs. Thus a lion cannot properly be considered to have fur at all, since fur, by definition, must be soft, fine, and thick. A lion's hairs are for the most part coarse and tend to be all of a size. They are also short, as befits an animal living in a hot climate. They lie flat against the skin, somewhat in the manner of the coat of a cow or horse, and they are nothing at all like the delicious deep coats of some of the other cats. Fine or coarse, the coat grows on a skin that is hung loosely on the cat's body. This loose skin is a great asset in fighting, for it can stand a great deal of pulling and tearing without damage to the tissues and organs that it covers.

This, then, is the architecture of cats. Considering their great differences in size (it takes about 50 average male house cats to equal the weight of one fully grown male lion), their distribution over all of the continents except Australia and Antarctica, and their adjustment to a wide variety of habitats—ranging from the snow-covered slopes and birch groves of the Himalayas to the sopping rain forests of Central America and the near-desert conditions of Equatorial Africa—cats are astonishingly alike. And it must be repeated that the reason for this similarity is that they are the nearest thing to a perfect

11

Black-footed Cat—14 inches, 7 pounds

European Wildcat
2 feet, 15 pounds

Lynx—3 feet, 60 pounds

stalking, hunting animal that the evolutionary process has yet produced.

The family trees of many types of animals are full of irritating gaps, and the branch that leads to cats from the primitive miacid carnivores is one such. There are very few catlike fossils lying about. Paleontologists have speculated that others may turn up in Asia, where all cats are believed to have originated. Despite the scarcity of fossils, this much is known: Cats of sufficient modernity to share the family Latin name of *Felidae* with today's species were certainly on the scene five million years ago and may have been in existence as long as ten million years ago. But even at that remote date there were already two distinct types. One group includes the ancestors of the quick, lithe cats of today. The other includes a somewhat heavier, presumably slower and more powerful type adapted to prey on the large and slow herbivores of the time. This branch of the family is epitomized by one of the most famous fossil creatures known to man, the Ice Age saber-toothed "tiger," or *Smilodon*.

The puzzle of the sabertooth began with the first discovery of its fossils and centered on the enormous fang development of the upper canines of this animal. In the largest sabertooths the fangs exceeded eight inches in length, forming a pair of curved daggers extending down from the upper jaw and, when the mouth was closed, even some distance below the bottom of the lower jaw. The question that was first asked about the sabertooth was: How did it get its jaw open wide enough to eat? Some theorists believe that this extraordinary animal became extinct because its teeth had grown too large to be manageable and it starved to death. This, of course, is ridiculous, for sabertooths of various kinds managed to get along with, and undoubtedly depended on, those oversized fangs for a period of nearly 40 million years.

So the puzzle about the sabertooth is not how it managed despite its scimitarlike teeth but how it used them. It is almost universally agreed today

Snow Leopard—7 feet, 100 pounds

Puma—8 feet, 200 pounds

Jaguar—7 feet, 400 pounds

Leopard—
8 feet, 200 pounds

that they were employed as stabbing weapons. Several sabertooths, the *Smilodon* of North America in particular, had enormously powerful necks and neck muscles, and the belief is that they killed with lethal downward thrusts of their giant canines. Other factors support this idea. For one thing, the lower jaw of the sabertooth was relatively weak and its ability to bite and tear somewhat limited. For another, the whole animal was large and heavily built, as if to give it the weight and leverage to make such an attack. The biggest sabertooths were larger than modern tigers and considerably heavier. Furthermore, there was an abundance of large prey animals prowling the earth in their heyday, of just the kind that a husky sabertooth might be able to handle. Many of these, like the young of mammoths, mastodons, and giant ground sloths, were large, slow, stolid animals weighing a ton or more. Like the sabertooths, they are now extinct, and it is reasonable to suppose that the predator followed the prey into oblivion.

What did survive is the less specialized branch of the cat family. Its members descend from an extinct ancestor called *Pseudaelurus*, which put in an appearance in Eurasia about 20 million years ago. *Pseudaelurus* was fairly small, about the size of a lynx or bobcat. It cannot have cut much of a figure alongside the more dramatic sabertooth, but it was quick and strong for its size, with equipment almost identical to that of modern cats, and it could live on smaller animals that a sabertooth could not catch. Gradually it evolved into three main lines: the Small Cats, ranging in size and variation from domesticated house cats to pumas; Big Cats, which include lions, tigers, leopards, and jaguars; and Cheetahs, which occupy a special branch on the feline family tree. In all, there are about three dozen species of cats that inhabit the earth today. It is with those species that survive in the wild that the rest of this book will concern itself.

Pallas' Cat—2 feet, 7½ pounds

Jaguarundi—3 feet, 20 pounds

Ocelot—3½ feet, 35 pounds

Clouded Leopard—5 feet, 50 pounds

Cheetah—
7 feet, 150 pounds

African Lion—9 feet, 500 pounds

Siberian Tiger—
12 feet, 700 pounds

Lions

Of all the wild animals with whom he shares the planet, one great cat—the lion—has always held supreme place in man's esteem and imagination. Ever since man began to observe the world about him and to think in symbols, he has honored the lion, crediting the regal beast with the attributes he prizes most in his own kind: nobility, courage, loyalty, combative skill, and sexual prowess. The ancient Egyptians used the lion as a symbol of divine power and kingly dignity. The Assyrians and Greeks represented the lion as keeping company with goddesses. In early Christian art the lion symbolized, variously, St. Mark, St. Jerome, and even Christ Himself, "the Lion of Judah." Later the lion, rampant and otherwise, found its way onto the coats of arms of many of the royal and noble families of Europe.

How did the lion acquire its kingly fame? Undoubtedly because it is in truth the most regal looking of animals. This attribution applies to both sexes, for a lioness is a creature of sinuous beauty. It is especially true, however, of the full-grown male, whose magnificent mane, not found on any other cat, ranging in color from rich golden to deep brown-black, marks him as a veritable monarch. And a lion's voice is as impressive as its looks. On a still night its roar can tingle the spine of a listener five miles away. In its behavior, too, the lion manifests the kingly virtues. Unless crossed in the quest for food or sex, it is majestically good-natured and gregarious.

Lions differ from all other cats in that they live and hunt in prides. The average pride consists of a number of lionesses and their cubs, a few young males, and, always, one dominant male. The leader of the pride may not be the largest or the strongest member, but his superiority is acknowledged by the other males, and they in turn are tolerated by the king. The size of a pride can vary considerably—from four or five members to 35 or more.

Among the big cats, the lion's only rival in size is the tiger. Dressed lion skins have been measured at more than twelve feet, but the average adult male in his prime is about nine feet long and weighs between 400 and 500 pounds. The female is smaller—about eight feet and 300 pounds. Alone among cats the male lion is clearly distinguishable from the female even at a distance because of his size and his great mane. Lions, whose lithe bodies are almost all muscle, are capable of prodigious physical feats. One swipe of a paw is enough to knock down a 600-pound zebra, and, despite their weight, lions are remarkable jumpers. One observer claims to have seen a male jump across a 36-foot-wide gorge; vertical leaps of 10 feet up banks or over hedges are made with ease. When lions are breeding they breed often. When a female is in heat the dominant male will mate with her every 20 or 30 minutes for hours at a time. A caged male and female in the Dresden Zoo are reported to have copulated 360 times in an eight-day period.

Once plentiful in Europe, the Near East, Middle East, and India, as well as Africa, the lion has been gradually swept back by the pastoral and, later, industrial encroachment of its chief enemy, man, until today the species is confined almost entirely to the great game preserves of East and South Africa; a scattered few Asian lions survive in the natural state in India's Gir Reserve. With the admirable exception of the establishment of the African reserves, man has done his best to eradicate the beast. The lion in its relationships with man appears to favor a policy of tolerant coexistence but will become a man-eater once it learns what easy prey the human animal can be. A historic example of lions acquiring a little too much of this dangerous knowledge was that of the man-eaters of Tsavo at the turn of the century: Two lions made off with and ate at least 28 workers on the Mombasa-to-Uganda railroad before being shot by the engineer in charge.

Some naturalists have challenged the male lion's vaunted nobility, pointing out that he lets the female do all the work in the hunt and then stuffs himself on the fruits of her work. This, however, may be more a matter of practicality than laziness. Because he is highly visible, the male lion is much more likely to alert and scare off prey than his more unobtrusive mate.

Aged and infirm lions are not protected by the pride but rather turned out to shift for themselves. Skinny and feeble, an old lion often ends its days being encircled, killed, and eaten by hyenas—an ignominious end for a monarch.

Lions are found in sub-Saharan Africa and, in limited numbers, in India (red). Lined areas are former distribution.

The Serengeti – A Lion's Paradise

Tanzania's protected 5,700-square-mile Serengeti National Park supports the densest lion population (about 1,000 animals) in the world. The reserve's rolling plains and savannas and huge migratory herds make it a perfect arena for a pride of lions to show off its hunting skills. In the Serengeti, tens of thousands of zebras and wildebeests are scattered for miles across the horizon, grazing, swatting flies with their tails, or just baking in the unrelenting sun. The sight of a pride of lions, observing the herd from a few hundred yards away, is an integral part of the picture.

The sharp eyesight of the antelope and its ability to outrun any lion make stalking by day on the open plain next to impossible for the cats. Instead they wait until nightfall. Then a vanguard of lionesses silently moves out one by one, circling around and behind the herd. If the males are cooperating, a few masculine grunts will send the herd stampeding toward the waiting females. Without the males, the lionesses must do the job on their own.

When wildebeests and zebras are plentiful they almost exclusively make up the lions' diet. A lion usually eats every two or three days but can, if necessary, survive for several weeks without eating at all. Going without food becomes a grave threat for some lions when the herds begin their seasonal migration across the plains. A lioness with a new litter of helpless cubs to care for may be stranded when the herd moves off and the rest of the pride leaves to follow it. Such a lioness, if desperate enough, may even take to man-eating. But more often, by stalking favored hunting places, such as a waterhole, and taking clues from other plains denizens, such as the vultures, even a lone huntress can succeed at a kill.

Some 300,000 bearded wildebeests, also called gnus, and zebras gather together on the vast, sun-scorched Serengeti Plain before beginning their seasonal migration to richer grazing grounds. These herds often travel distances of over 300 miles. During the height of the summer dry season many lions follow their food supply to the greener woodlands of the Serengeti.

16

Tricks of the Leonine Trade

A lioness, below, wise in the ways of the hunt, stealthily stalks her prey, using the underbrush as camouflage until she is ready to strike. For a free and easy meal, a lion will be on the lookout for vultures either circling in the sky or, as at left, perched in trees. They are always on hand when a kill is fresh and are telltale signals for a hungry cat. A lioness will wait, crouched and unmoving, in a thicket for as long as half a day until a group of wildebeests makes its move to a waterhole (right). A few unguarded moments as they lower their heads to drink give the lionesses enough time for a well-planned pounce.

A great variety of animals such as (from the top, above) zebras, baboons, nyalas, and giraffes will, at one time or another, turn up at the waterhole, making it a favorite stop on a feline's hunting rounds.

19

The Trials of a Lone Hunter

Stalking their prey as a team, a pride of lions can quickly and efficiently make a kill. In the sudden equatorial twilight a herd of zebras or wildebeests is spooked into a stampede and thunders through the line of waiting lionesses. Then it is short work for a lioness to pick off a startled victim, just as a cowboy selects a calf for branding in a roundup, bowl it over with a single blow, and pounce on its shoulders to deliver a death-dealing bite on the neck. Oftentimes, though, the first strike will not kill, for the lion is not a precision hunter like the cheetah or the leopard. In such instances, the lioness that brings down the prey will be joined instantly by her sisters. One might go for the throat, to choke the victim and prevent it from scrambling to its feet; another might attack the hindquarters, being careful to avoid the lethal hooves. In a matter of minutes the battle is over.

But when a lone mother lioness or an aged, weakened patriarch who has been expelled from the pride, or is too feeble to keep up with it, attempts to kill, the task becomes much more difficult and the chances of success much slimmer. It is not easy to fell a sturdy 600-pound zebra without the cooperation of the rest of the pride. Lone hunters do not have a long life expectancy, and all too often they end their days in the role of the hunted.

The thin, ravenous huntress miscalculated and missed her target—the zebra she is eying in the photograph above. Another, more experienced lioness (sequence at right) was luckier, although she nearly lost her quarry, too. Failing to get a lethal grip on the zebra, she had to struggle for nearly an hour before finally bringing it down. Afterward, the exhausted lioness did not touch her kill. Instead, she rested briefly, then trotted off for several miles to notify her pride that dinner was ready.

21

The Voracious Appetite of Lions

A hungry lion will devour almost any kind of meat, from that of a mouse to a hippopotamus. It has no finicky tastes or dietary taboos: Carrion seems as delectable to lions as freshly killed meat. On occasion, lions will eat their own kind. It is not unusual for a male lion, famished and irritable, to eat cubs. Although lions usually respect and avoid much bigger animals, they sometimes fearlessly attack and bring down large, dangerous beasts that might seem beyond their capacity to handle—such as a full-grown giraffe or a fierce 1,200-pound South African buffalo. If a carcass is big enough, a full-grown male can consume 50 to 60 pounds of meat at the first feeding and then polish off another 30 pounds at the next.

Sometimes, when stalking its prey, a lion may suddenly find that it is the pursued rather than the pursuer. The two lionesses at left had just killed a baby giraffe when the enraged mother appeared and, after a brief skirmish, sent them flying before her flailing hooves. When it comes to attacking other members of the cat family, lions have no inhibitions. The lone lioness at left, below, has somehow managed to bring down a much faster cousin, a cheetah, and is ready to dine. The best-laid plans for a group attack by a pride can sometimes be thwarted, as the film sequence at right, excerpted from Wild, Wild World of Animals, demonstrates. The wily wildebeest, confronted with a pride of stalking lionesses, darted back and forth until it found a break in the encircling line and raced through to open country, where it easily outdistanced them all. A less elusive member of the same herd, below, was not so fortunate.

Second Helpings

Lions obtain their food in three ways. They kill their own prey, scavenge from other predators, or eat animals that have died from disease or old age. Whether fresh or putrefied, large or small, killed or scavenged, a carcass is of great value, the means of survival to a lion. It is, however, equally sought after by other animals, such as hyenas, jackals, and vultures, and the lion must guard it constantly. A solitary predator rarely eats its kill alone without being disturbed by intruders, but a pride of lions can successfully fend off interlopers and guard a carcass long enough to get a second meal out of it.

Lions seem to follow a precise eating pattern. The prey's belly is ripped open and the heart, liver, and kidneys are eaten first. Next the remaining tissue or meat is devoured, hide, hair, and all. The dominant male of the pride, even if he played no part in the actual kill, is usually the first to eat. If game is abundant and the lion is feeling indulgent, the other cats of the pride may be allowed to join the feast. Otherwise they must wait until the male has had his fill before they can dig in. Cubs are fed last, if at all, and often it is the male lion who sees that they get even a few scraps.

They are used to periods of feast and famine, so cats gorge themselves when food is available. Five lions can polish off a 600-pound zebra in one day. Because a stuffed lion soon becomes sleepy, the jackals, vultures, and hyenas move in for whatever remains of the kill as soon as the pride lies down. A lion will try to chase the scavengers away, perhaps finally dragging the carcass into a nearby thicket. The contest can sometimes go on for hours, but eventually the drowsy cat simply gives in and lets the scavengers finish the contested kill.

Well aware that a 9,000-pound bull elephant will not detour around any living thing in its path, the lioness prudently carries off the remainder of her kill to a safer place in the savanna—one of the rare instances when the great cats will give ground to another creature.

Siesta Time

Lions sleep in the few puddles of shade or in the grass of the sun-warmed savannas for as much as 20 hours a day. Lazily self-confident, seemingly unaware of anything going on around them, the pride of lions below appears to be in a stupor, stretched out, motionless except for an occasional flick of a tail, bellies toward the sun, legs suspended in the air.

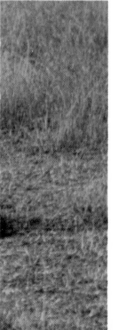

The cats above, in Manyara National Park, Tanzania, have gorged themselves on a fresh kill and are sleeping off the feast in the flowing branches of an acacia tree to escape the swarms of insects on the ground. Only with the setting of the afternoon sun can the stately figures of stalking lions once again be seen along the horizon.

They sat under a tree and smoked.

"Want to go back and speak to the Memsahib while we're waiting?" Wilson asked.

"No."

"I'll just step back and tell her to be patient."

"Good," said Macomber. He sat there, sweating under his arms, his mouth dry, his stomach hollow feeling, wanting to find courage to tell Wilson to go on and finish off the lion without him. He could not know that Wilson was furious because he had not noticed the state he was in earlier and sent him back to his wife. While he sat there Wilson came up. "I have your big gun," he said. "Take it. We've given him time, I think. Come on."

Macomber took the big gun and Wilson said:

"Keep behind me and about five yards to the right and do exactly as I tell you." Then he spoke in Swahili to the two gun-bearers who looked the picture of gloom.

"Let's go," he said.

"Could I have a drink of water?" Macomber asked. Wilson spoke to the older gun-bearer, who wore a canteen on his belt, and the man unbuckled it, unscrewed the top and handed it to Macomber, who took it noticing how heavy it seemed and how hairy and shoddy the felt covering was in his hand. He raised it to drink and looked ahead at the high grass with the flat-topped trees behind it. A breeze was blowing toward them and the grass rippled gently in the wind. He looked at the gun-bearer and he could see the gun-bearer was suffering too with fear.

Thirty-five yards into the grass the big lion lay flattened out along the ground. His ears were back and his only movement was a slight twitching up and down of his long, black-tufted tail. He had turned at bay as soon as he had reached this cover and he was sick with the wound through his full belly, and weakening with the wound through his lungs that brought a thin foamy red to his mouth each time he breathed. His flanks were wet and hot and flies were on the little openings the solid bullets had made in his tawny hide, and his big yellow eyes, narrowed with hate, looked straight ahead, only blinking when the pain came as he breathed, and his claws dug in the soft baked earth. All of him, pain, sickness, hatred and all of his remaining strength, was tightening into an absolute concentration for a rush. He could hear the men talking and he waited, gathering all of himself into this preparation for a charge as soon as the men would come into the grass. As he heard their voices his tail stiffened to twitch up and down, and, as they came into the edge of the grass, he made a coughing grunt and charged.

Kongoni, the old gun-bearer, in the lead watching the blood spoor, Wilson watching the grass for any movement, his big gun ready, the second gun-bearer looking ahead and listening, Macomber close to Wilson, his rifle cocked, they had just moved into the grass when

Macomber heard the blood-choked coughing grunt, and saw the swishing rush in the grass. The next thing he knew he was running; running wildly, in panic in the open, running toward the stream.

He heard the *ca-ra-wong!* of Wilson's big rifle, and again in a second crashing *carawong!* and turning saw the lion, horrible-looking now, with half his head seeming to be gone, crawling toward Wilson in the edge of the tall grass while the red-faced man worked the bolt on the short ugly rifle and aimed carefully as another blasting *carawong!* came from the muzzle, and the crawling, heavy, yellow bulk of the lion stiffened and the huge mutilated head slid forward and Macomber, standing by himself in the clearing where he had run, holding a loaded rifle, while two black men and a white man looked back at him in contempt, knew the lion was dead. He came toward Wilson, his tallness all seeming a naked reproach, and Wilson looked at him and said:

"Want to take pictures?'

"No," he said.

That was all any one had said until they reached the motor car. Then Wilson said:

"Hell of a fine lion. Boys will skin him out. We might as well stay here in the shade."

A Lion Family: A Matter of Pride

Every pride has one adult male (left) who, because of his dominance, is the leader of the group. As the king, he is the first to mate when the females are in heat and the first to feast when a kill has been made. In return, he guards the integrity of the pride, watching over the cubs while the lionesses are busy hunting and protecting the entire group from potentially dangerous intruders. Rarely will there be more than three adult males,in the family, for as the young cubs reach adulthood they will challenge the leader for his position. If they lose they are usually ousted from the clan and forced either to create their own prides or temporarily to lead a bachelor's life.

The lions' extraordinary sociability sets them apart from all other great cats. They hunt, eat, and rest together (above) in family groups called prides, which vary in size from as few as four members to as many as 30 or 40. The lionesses (left) form the core of the pride and assume the main hunting responsibility for the group. They are also in charge of the rearing of the cubs, who will suckle indiscriminately from any or all of the nursing females in the pride. Except for an occasional spat over food, pride members get along harmoniously, displaying warm signs of affection, such as licking one another's faces or rubbing cheeks when they meet.

The Looks of Love

The breeding period is a time for displays of affection between the mating couple, separated from the rest of the pride.

The actual act of copulation is a brief but lively encounter, with the male straddling the female from behind.

A courting lion is an attentive lion. For the lovesick-looking pair at left, as for all lions, the mating period begins when the female comes into heat. Unless she becomes pregnant, this will occur every three weeks. The mating couple separates from the rest of the pride and spends the five-day "honeymoon" in a secluded spot. During this time the cats are virtually inseparable. They walk together, sleep together, and even (at right) get a little bored together. Copulation, which occurs many times a day, takes place quickly and quietly except for an occasional growl when, in the height of passion, the male nips the female on the nape of the neck. Some males have been known to overreact during copulation, accidentally biting the lioness to death. More often, however, the breeding time is a romantic interlude in a lion's everyday routine.

The Rites of Eminent Domain

When a male lion establishes the territory of his pride, he marks it on bushes with a mixture of urine and a glandular secretion and proclaims it by roaring. Once established, a territory is inviolate, and the dominant lion is prepared to defend it to the death. The primary motivation for territoriality is sex. The leading male considers all the females in his pride to be his own property, and their hunting ground automatically becomes his territory. In areas where game is scarce, territorial limits may extend for ten miles in any direction; where the hunting is good, a lion's kingdom will be much smaller. Some lions that prey on migratory animals travel with the herds, like camp followers, and have no need or time to establish territories.

Prides and their territories are acquired by conquest. When one or more young males shows an interest in another's domain, it means war. Such intrusions are usually deliberate challenges to the local king. If the challenger is powerful enough to be a real threat, the battle for supremacy can be bloody indeed. It is not unusual for such a fight to end with both the intruder and the defender dead or dying. Similarly, lionesses will drive off any alien female that attempts to join the pride.

While male lions are not nearly so vigilant in patrolling their areas as other territorial animals, such as wolves, they do leave those olfactory warnings, and strange lions without the strength or courage to challenge a king will be forewarned and head the other way. It is not uncommon for one or two young "bachelor" lions to lurk around the limits of a marked territory, serving as grim reminders to the established leader of his own mortality.

Two compatible male lions of the same pride stand guard (left, top). Spotting trespassers, they quickly drive them off and watch their retreat (center). The established king thereupon urinates on a bush (bottom), an instinctive, almost ritualistic act that re-establishes his peaceable kingdom—until another challenger comes along.

The lion's roar is his awesome message to the world that he is lord and master of all he surveys. As an expression of territorial supremacy, roaring serves to warn any would-be intruders of his presence. A lioness uses a low-keyed, moaning roar to summon her cubs from hiding when she returns from the hunt or to locate other members of the pride when she becomes separated from them. When actually challenged, a mature lion snarls and growls as he fends off a brash young intruder (below) but roars only when he is letting the world know that he is king of the beasts—or, at least, of his own pride.

Under the silhouette of Mt. Kilimanjaro, a lone lioness sets out at dusk to begin her night's hunting. Solitary lionesses are unusual; most live and die within their pride and never leave the territory where they were born. Males, on the other hand, sometimes spend their entire adult lives as loners. Almost every male lion lives out his declining years as an outcast, exiled from the pride by a younger, stronger male and usually doomed to die hideously, eaten by hyenas. The cub above is destined for another kind of death. Weaned from her mother but too small to rate anything but leftovers from her greedy elders, she will die of starvation—a common fate among cubs.

43

Tigers

The largest, most awesome of the big cats is the tiger. Large males from Manchuria and Siberia grow to be more than 12 feet long and weigh more than 700 pounds. Subspecies in the tropical areas of its Asian range are smaller: Bengal tigers usually weigh no more than 500 pounds. Originally from the icy forests of Siberia, northern China, and Korea, the great striped cat migrated south across the Himalayas several million years ago and eventually reached much of India, the Malay Peninsula, Sumatra, Java, and Bali. For all its vast range, though, the tiger has become the rarest of cats. In India, the tiger population has shrunk from an estimated 20,000 a decade ago to fewer than 2,000 today. In Sumatra, Java, and Bali, the smaller, darker island species have virtually disappeared. Man's encroachments on the tiger's habitat and extensive hunting have brought the proud creature to the verge of extinction.

The tiger has an insatiable hunger for just about anything that crosses its path. A study of a population of Bengals disclosed a menu of three species of deer, wild oxen, domestic cows, water buffalo, monkeys, pigs, bears, lynxes, badgers, wolves, lizards, snakes, frogs, crabs, fish, locusts, termites, carrion, grass, and, rarely, soil. Tigers have been known to attack crocodiles, pythons, leopards, and even, when they are desperate for food, other tigers. Man-eaters are not unknown, although tigers and human beings usually coexist in the same communities with little or no concern for each other. When a man-eating tiger strikes, though, whole regions are paralyzed with fear until the killer is destroyed.

While the tiger's gaudy stripes make it a standout at any zoo or circus, they are a perfect camouflage in the elephant grass and brush where it stalks its prey. The orange and black color is darker in the smaller, tropical breeds of tiger. A solitary cat, the tiger will occasionally hunt alongside its mate, but that is strictly a temporary arrangement, restricted to the few weeks in winter or spring when tigers usually mate. Similarly, a tiger's territory, which he marks off with urine and proclaims with roars, is not a permanent home. After a few weeks, most tigers wander off to lead a nomadic life and mark off a new domain. In the wild, a tiger's life expectancy is reckoned at no more than 20 years, but with the pressures on the species today, a tiger

in less than prime condition with reflexes that are not at maximum efficiency is not likely to last even that long.

Most cats avoid the water, but tigers appear to enjoy bathing. In the southern reaches of their range they regularly take to the water when it is hot, and they swim very well.

The tiger stalks its prey using its natural camouflage and surrounding vegetation to approach within a few yards of its victim before knocking it over in a final rush. As with other big cats, the kill is made by biting the throat and frequently by breaking the neck. Hunting usually takes place at dusk or at night, but when it is hungry enough a tiger will break its nocturnal habits and rush a herd of antelope or other prey in broad daylight. Usually a silent hunter, the male tiger makes itself heard only when it is looking for a mate. Then it shatters the jungle night for hours with bloodcurdling roars until a willing tigress appears.

Tiger cubs, born blind and helpless in litters of two to four, are able to kill for themselves and hunt small game alone by the time they are 11 months old. They remain with their mothers, nevertheless, until they are about two. During this time, three or more tigers are sometimes seen together at a kill.

Many legends surround the tiger. One of the most persistent has been the story of the "jungle ghost," a white tiger. In 1951 the legend proved to be true when a white male was captured in the Indian district of Rewa. Mated to a normal tigress, he sired four normal black and orange cubs. Crossbred to one of his daughters, the white tiger begat three cubs, two of which were white with distinctive blue stripes. From this strange family a number of remarkable mutants have been developed.

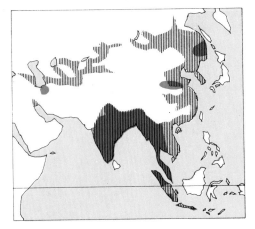

After its tiger census showed the alarming decline of the magnificent beast, the Indian government, in concert with several international conservation organizations, set up "Operation Tiger," establishing several specific tiger reserves. In these comparatively small areas the future of the great cat may be won or lost.

Tigers have a southern range from India to Bali and a northern range extending across the Himalayas north to Manchuria (red). In the past tigers roamed from Turkey to China (stripes).

The two major subspecies of tigers are the Siberian, at left, and the Bengal, below. The Siberian breed, sometimes called the Manchurian tiger, is the largest cat on earth. It ranges across 2,000 miles of the wastelands of northern Asia, as far north as the Arctic Circle, and is admirably adapted to the harsh weather of its world. The Bengal tiger is found throughout Southeast Asia and the central and southern parts of the Indian subcontinent. Smaller and more vividly marked than the Siberian cat, the Bengal crossed the Himalaya Mountains millions of years ago and gradually adapted to life in the tropics. The nearly extinct tigers of Indonesia are even smaller and darker than their mainland relations.

A Family Feast

Civilization's destruction of the forests and their wildlife in India has forced tigers to resort to preying on domestic herds of cattle and buffalo. This has earned them the reputation of being vicious and bloodthirsty pests, which has resulted in their being hunted to near extinction. The fact is, however, that tigers kill only in order to live.

To hunt successfully a tiger almost always waits until dark and then seeks out dense cover in which it can approach its prey unnoticed. Once a kill has been made, the cat often drags the carcass, sometimes over great distances, to water. Depending on the size of the catch, the tiger either finishes it off in one sitting, with frequent pauses for drinking, or guards it and dines on it repeatedly for days.

Although tigers occasionally share their kills with other tigers (as shown on these pages) they are, for the most part, solitary animals. They have distinct territories that they mark by spraying, defecating, and by leaving scratch marks on trees. The males, more than the females, guard these areas vigilantly, and they will not tolerate another male living in the vicinity. If, however, an intruder is just passing through, it is allowed to do so undisturbed.

When tigers live together for any prolonged period of time they are usually either a male and female cohabiting during the mating period, or a mother and her nearly grown offspring, or siblings who have left their mother but not yet one another. The male at right gives the coup de grâce to a buffalo he has just brought down for himself and his sisters (opposite page). The same tiger, above, gives in to his fatigue after his arduous task and the sumptuous feast that followed are over.

As soon as the male tiger killed the buffalo his three sisters, below and left, appeared, as if on cue, from the depths of the jungle darkness to help devour the carcass. Despite their blood-smeared faces the tigers exhibit laudable table etiquette, polishing off the meal in peace and harmony. As a rule female tigers will share their food with any tiger, male or female, that happens by. The more discriminating males will permit only females and cubs to join in.

THE TYGER

by William Blake

Tigers have captured the imaginations and stirred the fears of mankind since prehistoric times. Their elusive, secretive natures have created for them a mystic aura. In the late 18th century William Blake, the English poet, wrote—and illustrated—his famous tribute to the "tyger" and its hypnotic eyes, gleaming in the jungle.

The Tyger

Tyger Tyger. burning bright,
In the forests of the night :
What immortal hand or eye.
Could frame thy fearful symmetry?

In what distant deeps or skies
Burnt the fire of thine eyes!
On what wings dare he aspire?
What the hand, dare seize the fire!

And what shoulder, & what art,
Could twist the sinews of thy heart?
And when thy heart began to beat,
What dread hand? & what dread feet?

What the hammer? what the chain,
In what furnace was thy brain?
What the anvil? what dread grasp.
Dare its deadly terrors clasp!

When the stars threw down their spears
And water'd heaven with their tears:
Did he smile his work to see?
Did he who made the Lamb make thee?

Tyger Tyger burning bright
In the forests of the night:
What immortal hand or eye.
Dare frame thy fearful symmetry?

A Cat That Likes to Swim

All cats can swim if they are forced to, but most species carefully avoid the water except to drink. A few—notably the jaguar and the jaguarundi—will readily swim in pursuit of aquatic animals or fish. But only the tiger seems to relish bathing for its own sake. When they crossed the Himalayas thousands of years ago and moved into a tropical habitat, tigers discovered that the water was a convenient coolant. Now, in the steaming jungles of India, tigers take eagerly to the rivers and pools and sit or lie immersed to the neck, soaking and cooling off for hours at a time.

Stalking a Hartebeest

Graceful and swift, the leopard is an unqualified success as a hunter. It stalks its prey smoothly and silently, its sinewy leg and shoulder muscles primed for the single, lightning-fast leap that will place it, with little or no warning, on its victim. Leopards feast on animals that are plentiful in their area, such as the hartebeest (below), which will provide several meals. But not all hunts end with a successful kill. In the film sequence at right, a leopard climbs a tree that serves as an observation post, spots a bush pig in the grass, stalks its prey, breaks into full stride, almost catches the bush pig, manages to reach the pig and pulls it down in the grass. But in the final frames the bush pig escapes, heads for a nearby pond, and climbs the opposite bank to safety.

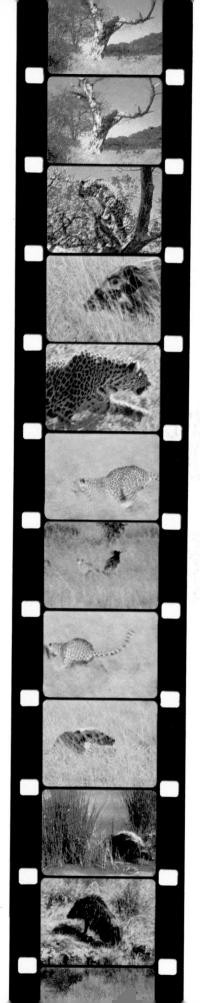

A freshly killed springbok is the evening meal for this leopard in Botswana in southern Africa. After stilling its initial hunger pangs with a few mouthfuls, the cat drags the carcass of its prey (usually baboons, warthogs, or antelopes but sometimes animals as large and unwieldy as young giraffes) into a tree. The leopard's catch is thus protected from scavenging jackals and hyenas, allowing the cat to return several times to finish off the remains.

60

a Passion in the Desert

by
Honoré de Balzac

Honoré Balzac (1799–1850)—the aristocratic de was adopted in his middle years—was one of the most prolific and esteemed titans of literature. His first novel made its appearance in 1830, and during the next 12 years Balzac turned out 79 lengthy novels, innumerable essays, and other literary works. The unfinished collection of interconnected novels and short novels, La Comédie Humaine, *a study of the French people of his time, represents Balzac's supreme literary effort. It is from a chapter, "A Passion in the Desert," of one of these collected novels (Scenes from Military Life) that the following excerpt comes. The protagonist of the story is a French soldier from Provence who is captured by Arabs while serving in Egypt and brought far into the desert. The soldier escapes his captors, taking a horse, a rifle, and a dagger. During his flight his horse dies, and the soldier wanders in the desert until he finds an oasis and a cave, where he falls asleep.*

In the middle of the night his sleep was troubled by an extraordinary noise; he sat up, and the deep silence around him allowed him to distinguish the alternative accents of a respiration whose savage energy could not belong to a human creature.

A profound terror, increased still further by the darkness, the silence, and his waking images, froze his heart within him. He almost felt his hair stand on end, when by straining his eyes to their utmost he perceived through the shadows two faint yellow lights. At first he attributed these lights to the reflection of his own pupils, but soon the vivid brilliance of the night aided him gradually to distinguish the objects around him in the cave, and he beheld a huge animal lying but two steps from him. Was it a lion, a tiger, or a crocodile? . . .

Presently the reflection of the moon, descending on the

62

horizon, lit up the den, rendering gradually visible and resplendent the spotted skin of a panther.

The lion of Egypt slept, curled up like a big dog, the peaceful possessor of a sumptuous niche at the gate of an hotel; its eyes opened for a moment and closed again; its face was turned toward the man. A thousand confused thoughts passed through the Frenchman's mind; first he thought of killing it with a bullet from his gun, but he saw there was not enough distance between them for him to take proper aim—the shot would miss the mark. And if it were to wake!—the thought made his limbs rigid. He listened to his own heart beating in the midst of the silence, and cursed the too violent pulsations which the flow of blood brought on, fearing to disturb that sleep which allowed him time to think of some means of escape.

Twice he placed his hand on his scimitar, intending to cut off the head of the enemy; but the difficulty of cutting the stiff, short hair compelled him to abandon this daring project. To miss would be to die for certain, he thought; he

preferred the chances of fair fight, and made up his mind to wait till morning; the morning did not leave him long to wait.

He could now examine the panther at ease; its muzzle was smeared with blood.

"She's had a good dinner," he thought, without troubling himself as to whether her feast might have been on human flesh. "She won't be hungry when she gets up."

It was a female. The fur on her belly and flanks was glistening white; many small marks like velvet formed beautiful bracelets round her feet; her sinuous tail was also white, ending with black rings; the overpart of her dress, yellow like unburnished gold, very lissome and soft, had the characteristic blotches in the form of rosettes, which distinguish the panther from every other feline species.

This tranquil and formidable hostess snored in an attitude as graceful as that of a cat lying on a cushion. Her blood-stained paws, nervous and well-armed, were stretched out before her face, which rested upon them, and from which radiated her straight, slender whiskers, like threads of silver. . . .

When the sun appeared, the panther suddenly opened her eyes: then she put out her paws with energy, as if to stretch them and get rid of cramp. At last she yawned, showing the formidable apparatus of her teeth and pointed tongue, rough as a file.

"A regular *petite maîtresse*," thought the Frenchman, seeing her roll herself about so softly and coquettishly. She licked off the blood which stained her paws and muzzle, and scratched her head with reiterated gestures full of prettiness. "All right, make a little toilet," the Frenchman said to himself, beginning to recover his gaiety with his courage; "we'll say good morning to each other presently," and he seized the small, short dagger which he had taken from the Mangrabins. At this moment the panther turned her head toward the man and looked at him fixedly without moving.

The rigidity of her metallic eyes and their insupportable luster made him shudder, especially when the animal walked toward him. But he looked at her caressingly, staring into her eyes in order to magnetize her, and let her

63

come quite close to him; then with a movement both gentle and amorous, as though he were caressing the most beautiful of women, he passed his hand over her whole body, from the head to the tail, scratching the flexible vertebrae which divided the panther's yellow back. The animal waved her tail voluptuously, and her eyes grew gentle; and when for the third time the Frenchman accomplished this interesting flattery, she gave forth one of those purrings by which our cats express their pleasure; but this murmur issued from a throat so powerful and so deep, that it resounded through the cave like the last vibrations of an organ in a church. The man, understanding the importance of his caresses, redoubled them in such a way as to surprise and stupefy his imperious courtesan. When he felt sure of having extinguished the ferocity of his capricious companion, whose hunger had so fortunately been satisfied the day before, he got up to go out of the cave; the panther let him go out, but when he had reached the summit of the hill she sprang with the lightness of a sparrow hopping from twig to twig, and rubbed herself against his legs, putting up her back after the manner of all the race of cats. Then regarding her guest with eyes whose glare had softened a little, she gave vent to that wild cry which naturalists compare to the grating of a saw.

"She is exacting," said the Frenchman, smilingly.

He was bold enough to play with her ears; he caressed her belly and scratched her head as hard as he could.

When he saw that he was successful, he tickled her skull with the point of his dagger, watching for the right moment to kill her, but the hardness of her bones made him tremble for his success. . . .

The soldier began to measure curiously the proportions of the panther, certainly one of the most splendid specimens of its race. She was three feet high and four feet long without counting her tail; this powerful weapon, rounded like a cudgel, was nearly three feet long. The head, large as that of a lioness, was distinguished by a rare expression of refinement. The cold cruelty of a tiger was dominant, it was true, but there was also a vague resemblance to the face of a sensual woman. Indeed, the face of this solitary queen had something of the gaiety of a drunken Nero: she had

satiated herself with blood, and she wanted to play.

The soldier tried if he might walk up and down, and the panther left him free, contenting herself with following him with her eyes, less like a faithful dog than a big Angora cat, observing everything, and every movement of her master.

When he looked around, he saw, by the spring, the remains of his horse; the panther had dragged the carcass all that way; about two-thirds of it had been devoured already. The sight reassured him.

It was easy to explain the panther's absence, and the respect she had had for him while he slept. The first piece of good luck emboldened him to tempt the future, and he conceived the wild hope of continuing on good terms with the panther during the entire day, neglecting no means of taming her, and remaining in her good graces.

He returned to her, and had the unspeakable joy of seeing her wag her tail with an almost imperceptible movement at his approach. He sat down then, without fear, by her side, and they began to play together; he took her paws and muzzle, pulled her ears, rolled her over on her back, stroked her warm, delicate flanks. She let him do whatever he liked, and when he began to stroke the hair on her feet she drew her claws in carefully.

The man, keeping the dagger in one hand, thought to plunge it into the belly of the too-confiding panther, but he was afraid that he would be immediately strangled in

her last conclusive struggle: besides, he felt in his heart a sort of remorse which bid him respect a creature that had done him no harm. He seemed to have found a friend, in a boundless desert; half unconsciously he thought of his first sweetheart, whom he had nicknamed "Mignonne" by way of contrast, because she was so atrociously jealous that all the time of their love he was in fear of the knife with which she had always threatened him.

This memory of his early days suggested to him the idea of making the young panther answer to this name, now that he began to admire with less terror her swiftness, suppleness, and softness. Toward the end of the day he had familiarized himself with his perilous position: he now almost liked the painfulness of it. At last his companion had got into the habit of looking up at him whenever he cried in a falsetto voice, "Mignonne."

At the setting of the sun Mignonne gave, several times running, a profound melancholy cry. "She's been well brought up," said the light-hearted soldier; "she says her prayers." But this mental joke only occurred to him when he noticed what a pacific attitude his companion remained in. "Come, *ma petite blonde*, I'll let you go to bed first," he said to her, counting on the activity of his own legs to run away as quickly as possible, directly she was asleep, and seek another shelter for the night.

The soldier waited with impatience the hour of his flight, and when it had arrived he walked vigorously in the direction of the Nile; but hardly had he made a quarter of a league in the sand when he heard the panther bounding after him, crying with that saw-like cry more dreadful even than the sound of her leaping.

"Ah!" he said, "then she's taken a fancy to me; she has never met any one before, and it is really quite flattering to have her first love." That instant the man fell into one of those movable quicksands so terrible to travellers and from which it is impossible to save oneself. Feeling himself caught, he gave a shriek of alarm; the panther seized him with her teeth by the collar, and, springing vigorously backward, drew him as if by magic out of the whirling sand.

"Ah!, Mignonne!" cried the soldier, caressing her enthusiastically; "we're bound together for life and death—but no jokes, mind!" and he retraced his steps.

From that time the desert seemed inhabited. It contained a being to whom the man could talk, and whose ferocity was rendered gentle to him, though he could not explain to himself the reason for their strange friendship. . . .

At last he grew passionately fond of the panther; for some sort of affection was a necessity.

Whether it was that his will, powerfully projected, had modified the character of his companion, or whether,

because she found abundant food in her predatory excursions in the desert, she respected the man's life, he began to fear for it no longer, seeing her so well tamed.

He devoted the greater part of his time to sleep, but he was obliged to watch like a spider in its web that the moment of his deliverance might not escape him, if any one should pass the line marked by the horizon. He had sacrificed his shirt to make a flag with, which he hung at the top of a palm tree, whose foliage he had torn off. Taught by necessity, he found the means of keeping it spread out, by fastening it with little sticks; for the wind might not be blowing at the moment when the passing traveller was looking through the desert.

It was during the long hours, when he had abandoned hope, that he amused himself with the panther. He had come to learn the different inflections of her voice, the expressions of her eyes; he had studied the capricious patterns of all the rosettes which marked the gold of her robe. Mignonne was not even angry when he took hold of the tuft at the end of her tail to count her rings, those graceful ornaments which glittered in the sun like jewelry. It gave him pleasure to contemplate the supple, fine outlines of her form, the whiteness of her belly, the graceful pose of her head. But it was especially when she was playing that he felt most pleasure in looking at her; the agility and youthful lightness of her movements were a continual surprise to him; he wondered at the supple way in which she jumped and climbed, washed herself and arranged her fur, crouched down and prepared to spring. However rapid her spring might be, however slippery the stone she was on, she would always stop short at the word "Mignonne." . . .

There was such youth and grace in her form! she was beautiful as a woman! the blond fur of her robe mingled well with the delicate tints of faint white which marked her flanks.

The profuse light cast down by the sun made this living gold, these russet markings, to burn in a way to give them an indefinable attraction.

The man and the panther looked at one another with a look full of meaning; the coquette quivered when she felt her friend stroke her head; her eyes flashed like lightning—then she shut them tightly.

"She has a soul," he said, looking at the stillness of this queen of the sands, golden like them, white like them, solitary and burning like them. . . .

The soldier relates how his strange friendship ended.

"You see, they ended as all great passions do end—by a misunderstanding. For some reason *one* suspects the other of treason; they don't come to an explanation through pride, and quarrel and part from sheer obstinacy. . . .

"I don't know if I hurt her, but she turned round, as if enraged, and with her sharp teeth caught hold of my leg—gently, I daresay; but I, thinking she would devour me, plunged my dagger into her throat. She rolled over, giving a cry that froze my heart; and I saw her dying, still looking at me without anger. I would have given all the world—my cross even, which I had not got then—to have brought her to life again. It was as though I had murdered a real person; and the soldiers who had seen my flag, and were come to my assistance, found me in tears." . . .

A Grim Drama in the Trees

The baboon, both as prey and adversary, is in continual conflict with the leopard. Alone and on the ground, the baboon is a slower-moving, doomed underdog in any encounter with the big cat. However, his chances of survival are better if it is daytime and if he can manage to get himself high enough into a tree, on limbs that will not support a leopard. In the sequence at right, a leopard, having sighted a branch-leaping baboon, climbs quickly up the tree in pursuit. But the thoroughly frightened baboon escapes momentarily by jumping to the ground and racing off. These photographs and the sequence shown on the next pages were taken under controlled conditions, employing different baboons. They show exactly how a leopard hunts and why it is such a formidable killer.

69

As every baboon knows, there is safety in numbers. While a lone baboon is easy game for an adult leopard, three or four adult males can drive a leopard off and are capable, in a group assault, of killing it. In the film strip at left a baboon bounds after a frightened leopard while his off-camera brethren follow. The leopard spots an acacia tree for a refuge where he can defend himself and climbs the tree while the rest of the baboon tribe catches up. In the frame above, the treed cat is at bay, surrounded by nattering baboons.

AFRICAN GENESIS

by Robert Ardrey

Robert Ardrey, successful screenwriter and playwright, created a furor in 1961 with the publication of his now famous book, African Genesis. His theories about man's animal ancestors developed from his observations of African animal behavior.

Below is an excerpt from this book, recounting the observations of the South African naturalist Eugène Marais, who watched a group of baboons for three years.

It was still dusk. The troop had only just returned from the feeding grounds and had barely time to reach its scattered sleeping places in the high-piled rocks behind the fig tree. Now it shrilled its terror. And Marais could see the leopard. It appeared from the bush and took its insolent time. So vulnerable were the baboons that the leopard seemed to recognize no need for hurry. He crouched just below a little jutting cliff observing his prey and the problems of the terrain. And Marais saw two male baboons edging along the cliff above him.

The two males moved cautiously. The leopard, if he saw them, ignored them. His attention was fixed on the swarming, screeching, defenceless horde scrambling among the rocks. Then the two males dropped. They dropped on him from a height of twelve feet. One bit at the leopard's spine. The other struck at his throat while clinging to his neck from below. In an instant the leopard disemboweled with his hind claws the baboon hanging to his neck and caught in his jaws the baboon on his back. But it was too late. The dying, disemboweled baboon had hung on just long enough and had reached the leopard's jugular vein with his canines.

Marais watched while movement stilled beneath the little jutting cliff. Night fell. Death, hidden from all but the impartial stars, enveloped prey and predator alike. And in the hollow places in the rocky, looming krans a society of animals settled down to sleep.

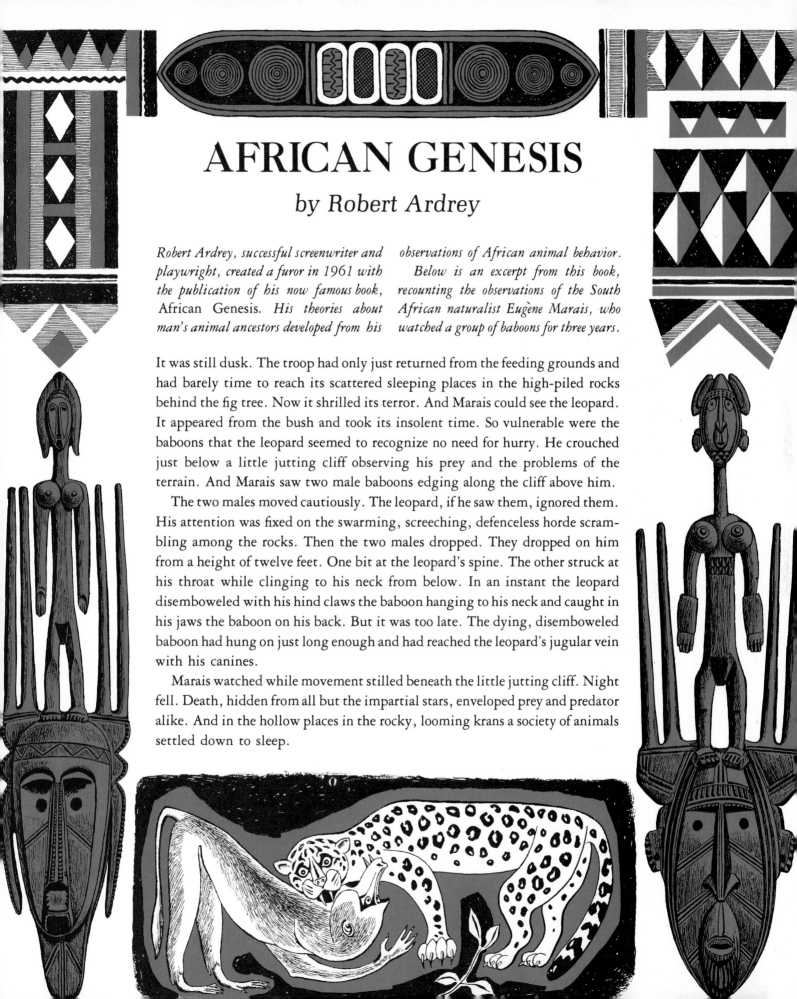

A Feline Masquerade

The magnificent snow leopard, or ounce, shown opposite in its frigid Himalayan fastness, is considered by many to be the most beautiful member of the cat family. Despite its spots and its name, the snow leopard is not a true leopard, but a separate species. A transition cat, it cannot be classified as either a Big Cat or a Small Cat, since it has characteristics of both and represents an evolutionary bridge between those two branches of the feline family. It lives in the highlands of the central Asian mountains and has been seen at elevations as high as 18,000 feet in the summer. The small, beautifully marked cat at left is another masquerader, the clouded leopard. Like the snow leopard, it travels under a misleading name and is also a transition cat. Soft-pelted, striped, and spotted, the clouded leopard is found in the densest forests of Southeast Asia and Indonesia. Primarily a tree-dweller, it is active in the early-morning hours and from late afternoon to evening, when it preys on small mammals and birds. A mature clouded leopard usually weighs just under 50 pounds, but its long canine teeth and powerful build make it an outstanding hunter.

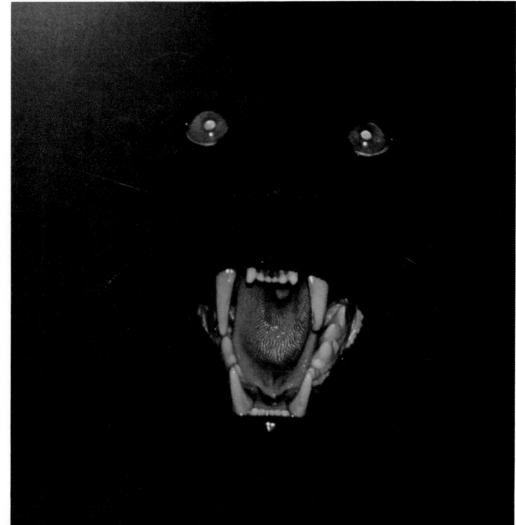

The ferocious-looking black panther at left is a misnamed, mutant member of the leopard family, although until recently it was believed to be a separate species. Close examination disclosed that it has a true leopard's spots, in an almost invisible black-on-black pattern. It occurs in Africa and Asia wherever conventional leopards are found. It is not a subspecies: black and spotted leopards occur in the same litters, and black leopards will readily mate with spotted members of the family.

Lions, Gorillas and

Carl Akeley, the famous American naturalist, was on a collecting expedition in Africa for the American Museum of Natural History in New York when he had a horrifying encounter with a leopard. In the arid back country of Somalia he shot a warthog, whose head he wanted for the museum, and left it in the brush to be picked up later in the day. When he returned at sundown the warthog carcass had disappeared. Searching for it, Akeley noticed something moving behind a bush and, without making certain what it was, fired his gun blindly into the bush. An explosion of coughs informed him that he had shot a leopard. In the gathering darkness Akeley prudently decided to leave matters as they were and to return the next day.

After stumbling across a dry riverbed, he climbed the riverbank and looked back. To his dismay he found that the wounded cat was following him. In a panic, he emptied his gun, momentarily stopping the leopard. But before he could reload his gun, the leopard leaped up the riverbank and sprang at him. Akeley's account of what happened is excerpted from his book Lions, Gorillas and Their Neighbors.

"Immediately I was face to face with the leopard in midair. My trusty rifle was knocked flying from my hands and in my arms was the leopard—eighty pounds of furious bloodthirsty cat. I knew she intended to sink her teeth into my throat and hold me tight in the grip of her jaws and forepaws while with her hind paws she dug out my stomach—for this practice is the pleasant way of leopards. But unexpectedly enough and most happily for me, she missed her aim. Instead of clutching my throat she struck me high in the chest and caught my upper right arm in her mouth. Thus not only was my throat saved but her hind legs were left hanging clear where she could not reach my stomach.

"With my left arm I seized her throat and tried to wrench my right arm free, but this I could do only little by little. When I got grip enough on her throat to loosen her hold just a bit, she would seize and set her jaws again in my arm an inch or two further down. In this way, I drew the full length of my arm inch by inch through her slavering poisonous mouth. During all this time I was not conscious of any pain whatsoever but only of the sound of the crushing of tense muscles and the choking, snarling grunts of the infuriated beast. As I pushed her jaws farther and farther down my arm, I bent over and finally, when my arm was almost free, I fell to the ground—the leopard underneath me. My right hand was now in her mouth, my left hand clutched her throat, my knees were on her chest, my elbows in her armpits which spread her front legs so far apart that her frantic clawing did nothing more than tear my shirt. Here we both struggled for life, man and beast. We were both determined to die hard. The leopard writhed and twisted her body in an effort to get hold of the ground and turn herself over, but the loose shifting sand offered her no hold or purchase. . . .

"Now during all this time, my original state of abject, helpless terror had changed utterly into one of complete

Their Neighbors
by Carl Akeley

physical anesthesia and of the greatest mental activity. All dread of death had vanished and the only sense of physical hurt I had at all was toward the end, when with my hand shoved down her throat, my thumb was pinched by the animal's molars. . . . I continued to shove my right hand down her throat so far and so hard that she could not close her jaws. With my other hand I gripped her throat in strangle hold. Then I surged down hard upon her with my knees, putting all the power in them I could muster. To my surprise I felt a rib break. I began to feel sure of myself. I did it again. Another rib cracked. Then I felt her relax, a sort of easing up and letting go, though she continued to struggle. Now at the same time I felt myself weakening in like manner. I had done my utmost. Soon it would become a question as to which one would give up first. But I resummoned my failing strength and held on to the big cat and thrust my knees down on her chest again. Little by little her struggling ceased. The fight was finished. *My strength had outlasted hers.*"

Jaguars

The jaguar is the biggest, most powerful, and most feared feline of the Western Hemisphere. It is a formidable animal, and it is not surprising that the jaguar is known in the Spanish- and Portuguese-speaking lands of Latin America that it inhabits as the *tigre*. The word "jaguar" is derived from an ancient Indian name, *yaguar*, which is said to mean "the killer which overcomes its prey in a single bound."

Fully developed male jaguars reach an overall length of more than seven feet. But although it has been hunted and killed—and presumably weighed—by man for centuries, estimates of the jaguar's maximum weight vary widely, from 250 to 400 pounds. Spotted like the leopard but with larger rosettes on a rich yellow or tawny background, the jaguar is easily distinguishable from its Old World cousin by its larger head, more compact form, and more powerful paws. It shares with the lion, the tiger, and the leopard the ability to let loose a hair-raising roar that wakes the jungle and sends its inhabitants scurrying in terror. This is one of the characteristics that distinguishes Big Cats from Small Cats, which can only purr and yowl.

The jaguar will pursue almost any kind of animal prey within its range, the favorite items in its diet being the peccary, a New World relative of the wild pig, and the 100-pound capybara, the largest of all the rodents. Both are plentiful and easily killed. Also favored are river reptiles, including the caiman, a Latin American alligator. The jaguar jumps the caiman along the shore, killing it by breaking its neck, and then proceeds to tear open its thick, armorlike hide. In the same way, the great cat will pounce on a turtle, turn it over, and rip it out of its shell. Omnivorous in its taste, the jaguar will even leave the jungle and venture onto a beach to dig turtle eggs out of the sand.

A strong swimmer and agile climber, the jaguar pursues its prey into lakes and rivers and to the upper branches of trees. It is a fast runner but tires quickly over long distances and therefore seems an unlikely choice for the name of a well-known British car that presumably is not only speedy but is also built to stand up over the long haul.

The jaguar will sometimes attack and carry off domestic stock, especially pigs and calves. It will even occasionally overcome its wariness of man by entering huts to snatch dogs, children, and old people. There is considerable disagreement among the experts as to whether individual jaguars become man-eaters, as renegade lions, tigers, and leopards sometimes do. It appears more likely that the jaguar has learned from generations of experience that man is to be avoided, although when cornered the big cat will not hesitate to attack the men and dogs who hunt it for its valuable pelt. The jaguar's only rival for size in the Western Hemisphere is the puma or cougar, but the jaguar is heavier, stronger, and has a more massive head.

Once found as far north as California, New Mexico, Arizona, and Texas, the jaguar today has not been encountered on the United States side of the Rio Grande for more than 25 years. The most recent sightings were in Arizona, New Mexico, and Texas in the late 1940s. The cat is still hunted extensively in Mexico and Central America, but the greatest concentrations and the biggest specimens are found in the jungles of the Mato Grosso of Brazil.

Like many animals whose range is primarily in subtropical and tropical areas, the jaguar appears to have no definite breeding period and will mate at any time of the year. The female's gestation period is about 100 days, and she produces a litter of from two to four. The kittens are fed and protected until they are about a year old and able to shift for themselves. They remain with their mother until the age of two, and they reach sexual maturity at three. Their lifespan in captivity ranges up to 20 years.

In the pre-Columbian civilizations of Peru, Central America, and Mexico, the jaguar was worshipped as a god. Artists of the early Chavin Culture of Peru, about 1000 B.C., fashioned stone idols of deities represented as part man and part jaguar. At the same time, 1,700 miles to the north, stone images of the jaguar-god made their appearance in southern Mexico. Since no evidence of any communication between the widely separated civilizations has been found, the coincidence is a puzzle for archaeologists. It is a tribute to the jaguar's capacity to stir the minds of humans that this handsome cat served as the unifying religious symbol of supernatural strength and power for both of the first two successful civilizations of America.

The jaguar population (red) extends from the U.S.–Mexico border through most of Central and South America.

A Solitary Amphibious Hunter

The jaguar is the only one of the New World cats that has the ability to roar. That deep and awesome sound is a warning to all the wild creatures that hear it because, once an animal is stalked by a jaguar, there are few places where it can go to elude the cat's powerful assault. A skillful and ready swimmer, a jaguar will unhesitatingly leap into a river to pursue an alligator or turtle. Monkeys in trees scatter in fear when they sense the nearness of the magnificent cat, for, rather than an obstacle, the branches present a

stage on which the jaguar can perform its impressive climbing and leaping feats.

Although the jaguar's prey includes rodents and reptiles, fishes and birds, its taste for domestic animals, such as cattle or horses, has earned it the wrath of man. Packs of dogs have been used to track the cat, which will instinctively take to the trees, where it can easily be shot. Others, however, have been known to stand their ground and defend themselves, attacking anyone, dog or man.

At the water's edge a jaguar can usually find a good meal, if it has the skill to get it. The young cat at right, however, hasn't yet learned that the capybara cowering in the reeds is his for the taking. Instead he pokes at the rodent with curiosity, giving the animal time to gather its courage and flee. The older and wiser jaguar below wastes no time in pursuing its prey and, with Olympic form, leaps after it into a plant-choked pond.

Pumas

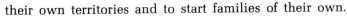

By any of its many names—puma, mountain lion, cougar, panther, or a dozen others—the American version of the lion looks very much like its African cousin minus its majestic mane. A handsome cat, the puma was once the most widely distributed and still has the widest north-south distribution of all mammals in the New World, ranging from southern Canada to Tierra del Fuego at the tip of South America. Over this 8,000-mile, two-continent spread the puma makes itself at home in steaming jungles, arid sub-deserts, swamplands, or up to 10,000 feet in the forested areas of mountains.

A mature puma may measure eight feet from its nose to the tip of its tail, and an occasional specimen, usually from a cold, mountainous region, may weigh more than 200 pounds. Among American cats, only the shorter, heavier-bodied jaguar weighs more. Pumas inhabiting lowlands are smaller than upland strains, some less than six feet long and weighing only a hundred pounds. Typical of cats, females are about a third smaller than males.

A lithe and agile athlete, the puma, although it doesn't take readily to water, is an accomplished swimmer and climber. It has been seen to drop 40 to 50 feet from a tree without hurting itself, leap 25 feet from a standstill after its prey. In Central and South America, where their habitats meet, pumas and jaguars are instinctive enemies, but a puma can almost always elude the more powerful jaguar because of its superior speed and agility.

The sleek coat of the yellow-eyed puma may be tawny to grayish, depending on its habitat, but it is always a solid color, with white on the chest, throat, and belly. Dusky patches border the white upper lip and the back of the ears, and the tip of the tail is black.

Pumas are loners except at mating time, when a pair will stay together for about two weeks. Three months later, in a rocky den or some other secluded hideaway, the female gives birth to from one to six cubs, their coats distinctly spotted with black and their tails ringed. Until their eyes open they stir only enough to nurse, but when they are two weeks old they are bright-eyed and playful. By the time they are a year old they are nearly four feet long and weigh almost 50 pounds. The spots fade from their coat as they mature. Cubs usually stay with their mother for two years before breaking away to create their own territories and to start families of their own.

In North America the puma was once found from coast to coast. By 1900 it had been nearly exterminated or forced to retreat from eastern regions. A remnant population of no more than a hundred isolated animals persists today in the Everglades. And there are still reports of pumas being sighted in New England and even in New Jersey. Today, the last North American stronghold for the puma is in Mexico and the rugged country of the western United States and Canada.

Pumas usually hunt on the ground, but they will nimbly pursue their prey up trees if necessary. In mountains or open-range country they prowl during the day when their prey is also feeding. In lowland tropical regions, where most animals are active at night, the adaptable puma becomes nocturnal too. Where they themselves are hunted, pumas will venture out only after dark. A big male may roam 20 or 25 miles in a single night of hunting.

Pumas are stealthy stalkers. When close to their prey, they rush and then pounce, generally knocking their victim down with a lightning-like bite on the nape of the neck. A favorite quarry in North America is the white-tailed deer. In settled areas the puma is known as a "varmint" because of its forays on domestic livestock.

After a puma has eaten its fill, it buries the remains of its kill under brush or snow. The next day the cat will come back to eat more, and it may return for a third meal. It does not confine its meals to large animals, however, and will eat mice or even grasshoppers.

Stories of pumas attacking and killing men have been grossly exaggerated. They will usually attack men only when treed or cornered where there is no escape. Many pumas have been kept in zoos and other wildlife exhibits where they breed successfully and may live for 15 years or longer.

Despite its reputation as a yowler, the puma is a quiet cat. Even when trapped or harried by baying hounds it generally remains silent. Most of the screams attributed to pumas can be traced to the eerie screech of a barn owl or some other source. But occasionally the puma, usually during mating, does indeed let loose a scream, an unforgettable, blood-curdling sound in the night.

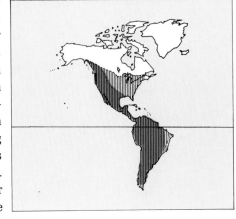

Pumas once roamed North and South America (stripes). Present range is shown in red.

A Fight with a Mother Panther

by James Fenimore Cooper

The first American novelist to capture the imagination of readers in all parts of the world, the aristocratic James Fenimore Cooper (1789–1851) saw his works published, it was reported, "in 34 places in Europe as soon as he produces them." The extent of Cooper's popularity was such that in 1888 the famous Austrian composer Franz Schubert pleaded from his deathbed for another Cooper novel to distract him in his mortal illness.

Cooper's first successful work was The Spy *(1821), a historic novel that centered on the American Revolution. He also turned out sea stories, satires, and even a history of the American Navy, but his most famous work was a series of five frontier romances, known collectively as* The Leatherstocking Tales. *These novels—*The Pioneers *(1823),* The Last of the Mohicans *(1826),* The Prairie *(1827),* The Pathfinder *(1840), and* The Deerslayer *(1841)—have best stood the test of time and remain popular today.*

It is from one of The Leatherstocking Tales—The Pioneers—*that the following excerpt is taken. It describes, in typical Cooper prose, a dramatic confrontation between man and beast. Elizabeth and Louisa are walking in a thickly wooded, mountainous area, accompanied by Elizabeth's dog, Brave. Suddenly the still air is punctuated by strange, mournful cries.*

"Listen! there are the cries of a child on this mountain! Is there a clearing near us, or can some little one have strayed from its parents?"

"Such things frequently happen," returned Louisa. "Let us follow the sounds; it may be a wanderer starving on the hill."

Urged by this consideration, the females pursued the low, mournful sounds, that proceeded from the forest, with quick and impatient steps. More than once, the ardent Elizabeth was on the point of announcing that she saw the sufferer, when Louisa caught her by the arm, and pointing behind them, cried:

"Look at the Dog!"

Brave had been their companion, from the time the voice of his young mistress lured him from his kennel, to the present moment. His advanced age had long before deprived him of his activity; and when his companions stopped to view the scenery, or to add to their bouquets, the Mastiff would lay his huge frame on the ground and await their movements, with his eyes closed, and a listlessness in his air that ill accorded with the character of a protector. But when, aroused by this cry from Louisa, Miss Temple turned, she saw the Dog with his eyes keenly set on some distant object, his head bent near the ground, and his hair actually rising on his body, through fright or anger. It was most probably the latter, for he was growling in a low key, and occasionally showing his teeth, in a manner that would have terrified his mistress, had she not so well known his good qualities.

"Brave!" she said, "be quiet, Brave! What do you see, fellow?"

At the sounds of her voice, the rage of the Mastiff, instead of being at all diminished, was very sensibly increased. He stalked in front of the ladies and seated himself at the feet of his mistress, growling louder than before, and occasionally giving vent to his ire by a short, surly barking.

All in the Family

Because they hunt in the daylight hours, it is not unusual to see a mother cheetah and a number of nearly grown cubs traveling together, as in the group above. Cheetahs are fairly competent hunters by the time they are a year old but usually remain with their mother for another four or five months. Mature males tend to travel singly, joining the females only at mating time. Recently zookeepers have bred cheetahs in captivity for the first time by following the natural system and keeping the two sexes apart until the female comes into heat. When they were kept in the same enclosure and allowed to live together year round, the cats invariably refused to mate. At left are three affectionate young adolescents from the same family.

Four partially concealed cheetah cubs peer through the tall grass (below), intently watching a distant herd. Because of their disproportionately small heads and other marked differences—the shape of their heads, the length and musculature of their legs, their blunted claws—it is obvious that cheetahs evolved separately, and they are recognized as a distinct breed of cat, separate from the other two principal branches of the feline family, the Big Cats and the Small Cats.

Survival of

With its disproportionately long legs, the cheetah is more nearly vertical than other large cats when it sits up (left). In action, though, those seemingly ungainly legs can propel a cheetah at its incredible top speed for about a quarter of a mile. But the race does not always go to the swiftest. In the photograph below, a tame cheetah was released to chase a herd of impalas. As it turned out, the cheetah's timing was off, it failed to get a good jump on the fleet-footed impalas, and they all escaped.

the Fleetest

Four-footed animals almost all move in the same way, as illustrated by the drawing below of a cheetah and a horse. If the left forefoot begins the motion, it is followed by the right hindfoot. The right forefoot advances next. The left hindfoot completes the cycle, followed by the left forefoot, which begins it again. Although the cheetah has shorter legs than the horse, it can outrun it over short distances. This is because its extremely supple back permits the cat's powerful hind legs to move far ahead with each stride.

A. Singer

Inevitably, vultures materialize at a kill, and their insatiable greed makes them so bold as to threaten two cheetahs feasting on a victim (top left). But the birds are easily routed by one of the pair (left), and the vultures and their bravado quickly vanish.

The final moments of a successful hunt have been frozen in the film sequence at the extreme left. A lone cheetah picks out a Thomson's gazelle from a herd in the savanna and speeds after it. The cat wheels around as the small antelope desperately zigzags, swerves to one side, and is finally overwhelmed in a cloud of dust. In the photograph at left, the cheetah crouches over its prey just before devouring it.

101

Lynxes and Bobcats

His haughty stare, the stiff ruff that frames his pale face, and his elegantly tufted ears give the lynx the appearance of some feline grandee out of an El Greco portrait. Other parts of the Northern or Canadian lynx—disproportionately long, muscular hind legs, an abbreviated tail, and huge, thickly furred paws—do not fit the aristocratic picture. They are, however, excellent adaptations to the cat's harsh northern habitat, enabling a 40-pound lynx to move easily and quickly across the softest snow in pursuit of its favorite prey, the snowshoe hare. And those tufted ears that distinguish the lynx from most other cats are not merely decorative tassels: They function as hearing aids, antennae that increase the animal's ability to detect the slightest sound. If the tufts are cut off, the lynx's keen sense of hearing goes into a marked decline.

Among the most widely distributed of all cats, the lynx (opposite) inhabits subpolar forest lands around the world. In North America, lynxes range from the Alaskan tree line as far south as the mountains of Colorado. A subspecies, the brightly dappled Spanish lynx, once ranged all over the Continent but is now an endangered animal, restricted to Portugal, southern Spain, and remote fastnesses in the Carpathian Mountains. The lynx's range and its numbers have been steadily shrinking through settlement and cultivation of the land and through the depredations of hunters and trappers. The thick pelts with their luxuriant, frosty guard hairs are highly valued in the fur trade and the fashion industry. Lynxes cherish them too, but their hides may be their undoing.

An elusive creature who is most active in early morning and late afternoon, the lynx usually hunts alone and avoids the company of other lynxes except during the mating season, January to March, when their woodland habitats become a bedlam of the yowling love calls of tom lynxes. They live and hunt in territories in which significant places like caves, rock piles, and trees are marked by droppings and claw marks. The territories are not sacrosanct, however, as far as male lynxes are concerned. They will tolerate the intrusion of other toms, although they will avoid contact with each other. Females are not so agreeable. On the rare occasions when a strange female blunders into another's territory, a cat fight almost inevitably follows, with the intruder hightailing it to friendlier regions.

The North American lynx will prey on almost anything that moves, but its almost exclusive game is the snowshoe hare. In Scandinavia reindeer are the principal food. But in that bitterly cold climate the cadavers freeze quickly, and lynxes, unable to cope with deep-frozen meat, can rarely get more than one quick meal from a victim.

While the Northern lynx has retreated from civilization, its smaller, look-alike cousin, the bobcat, or wildcat, has increased in number as man has cleared the wilderness and can be found in all of the original 48 states, southern Canada, and northern Mexico. Bobcats prefer open country to the protective forests, and, unlike lynxes, they have learned to coexist with man. They are not afraid to steal into a farmyard to get a young lamb or an entire flock of chickens, a trait that has put them next to the coyote and puma on farmers' and ranchers' pest lists.

The bobcats' breeding season occurs in winter, and, like the lynxes, their caterwauling courtship makes the earth tremble. Both bobcats and lynxes are excellent swimmers and climbers, and their climbing skill has often led to their death. Once treed, a cat is an easy target for a hunter.

Because they live in a less rigorous climate than their northern cousins, bobcats are not equipped with the padded snowshoe paws of lynxes, and their fur is not as luxuriant and warm. While bobcat fur is of little or no commercial value, the cats are still widely hunted in areas where they are a menace to farm animals. There are differences of opinion as to just how serious the bobcat's depredations really are. By preying on weak, injured, or aged members of deer herds, the cats may be performing a service by thinning out the weaker members and helping to maintain a good, healthy breeding herd. Nevertheless, in the eleven states where there is a bounty on them, bobcat pelts are worth as much as $35. Still, the bobcat seems to have an instinct for survival that will assure him of a place in the world when the bigger cats may have vanished.

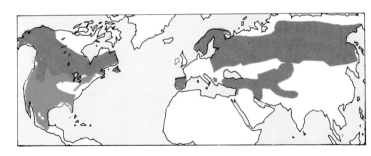

Lynxes (blue) range over subpolar regions around the world. A subspecies, the Spanish lynx, is found in Iberia. Bobcats (red) occur only in North America.

102

The four lynx kittens above have one another for company in their well-concealed den while their mother, probably looking very much like the stalking Spanish lynx at right, is off hunting for their evening meal.

Mother's Gone Hunting

Sometime around its first birthday a lynx becomes sexually mature. During the height of the mating period, which occurs in the months of late winter and early spring, the quiet of the woodlands is broken by the high-pitched caterwauling of courting lynxes . Fifty to 60 days after she conceives, the female lynx gives birth to a litter of two to four cubs. When they are born, the kittens are blind and helpless little creatures weighing only about 12 ounces each. Until they are weaned, about two months after their birth, they must rely completely on their mother for food and protection. This is why litters are seldom born during the height of winter, from November through January, when hunting conditions are at their worst and lone lynxes have all they can do to keep themselves fed.

The Bobcat: A Lynx Lookalike

The bobcat is North America's most common wild cat, found in southern Canada, Mexico, and most of the United States. Its habitat is continental, from the swamps of the Southeast to the rocky snow-covered regions of the Northwest and to the arid canyons of the Southwest. The cat has keen eyesight and sensitive hearing, although its ear tufts are much smaller than the lynx's. In the colder northern and mountain regions its substantial paws are thickly furred. These built-in snowshoes allow the bobcat to bound quickly over the softest snow after a hare. Bobcats also prey on larger animals such as deer, though usually they will attack only the young and sick and bring these down by pouncing on them from the branches of a tree.

Bobcats are territorial animals and mark their areas by spraying and scratching trees. Their ranges expand and diminish in inverse proportion to the abundance of prey found within their boundaries. They are also creatures of habit. They have favorite ledges and trees to sit in (right) and trails that, once established, they will use again and again. This can sometimes prove fatal to the bobcat, for veteran hunters who spot a cat sitting in a tree or prowling along a trail have only to wait until it returns to get an unsporting shot at it.

Because bobcats often live near farmlands they are known to take such livestock as sheep, goats, and calves. They also eat the animals caught in traps set by hunters. Usually, however, bobcats avoid confrontations and keep out of sight, especially in the presence of man.

A quick glance at the bobcat at left makes it easy to see why these solitary and elusive animals are so often confused with their lynx cousins, but a closer examination reveals the differences. The bobcat has a longer tail, shorter legs with smaller, less thickly furred paws and less visible ear tufts. Although bobcat kittens (like the one above, being protected by its fierce-looking mother) are the same size as baby lynxes at birth, they grow into smaller adults weighing only 15 to 25 pounds at maturity.

The snow-carpeted forestland of Castle Creek in Colorado is a mealtime heaven for the bobcat pictured on these pages. Rodents of all kinds, as well as the snowshoe hare, are the bobcat's favorite prey, and on this particular day the rabbits are out in abundance. The cat above wastes no time getting on the trail of a fleeing hare. Stalking its prey (right) is a time-consuming process that requires a bobcat's full concentration, for if it miscalculates its distance and attacks too soon, the swifter rabbit will almost always get away.

110

Once the bobcat gets within 40 feet of the luckless snowshoe hare, it launches its attack. Accelerating to full speed, it moves to within inches of its target, ready to pounce. The rabbit, however, suddenly wheels around (right) and runs past the startled bobcat. This strategy wins the hare only a few extra moments. The bobcat soon catches up with it, and with a forceful swipe of the cat's paw the rabbit is thrown in the air and the contest is ended.

Servals and Caracals

Like their larger and smaller brethren, the middleweight servals and caracals are marvels of feline design, both in the beauty of their markings and in the sheer efficiency of their physical equipment. It is as though nature had decreed that cats will come in many sizes and colors but each will be individually adapted to the environment it inhabits.

A prime example of this rule of natural adaptation is the handsomely spotted serval. Native to Africa, south, north, and east of the Sahara, it lives in thick grass and bushy cover near streams, lakes, and marshes. It feeds on cane rats, mice, hares, lizards, guinea fowl, francolin and other fast-flying game birds, small tree-dwellers like the hyrax, and even the young of the smallest antelopes. Hunting such a variety of prey in such a habitat, the serval must have some very specialized equipment: keen hearing to detect rodents moving unseen in the silent depths of the grassland, sufficient height to spot winged quarry over the top of the grass, and the speed and skill to catch agile small game. And that is precisely the equipment the serval has. It is long-legged, tall and slender (about three feet long, weighing 30 to 35 pounds), and very fast. Its ears are so preposterously large that they almost spoil the aesthetics of its form, but with them it can detect the vibrations of a mouse's shudder. On its long legs it bounds through the grass in a series of energetic but graceful leaps. It can catch a bird in flight or nip quickly up a tree to surprise a hyrax in its arboreal lair. The serval's acrobatics in the tall grass, most naturalists agree, are a tactical trick to flush the hare or other rodent that may be lying low in the deep cover. And once flushed or even detected in the slightest movement, the smaller animal is doomed.

The caracal (opposite) also has a pair of remarkable ears. They are black—the word *caracal* means "black-eared" in Turkish—and tapered off in lynxlike tufts that can either flop over rakishly or bristle alertly. Because of its ears and long, muscular hindquarters, the caracal is sometimes called the African lynx, but although the two cats are closely related, the caracal is classified as a distinct species. Certainly it is one of the handsomest members of the feline family, with a sleek, unpatterned reddish-brown coat and soft underbelly that is sometimes speckled with brown spots. Its cold, arrogant eyes glitter like emeralds.

In India and Iran the caracal has been tamed and trained to hunt, like the cheetah. With the smaller caracal, though, the prey is more likely to be birds than the larger antelopes that trained cheetahs stalked. Birds are a staple of the caracal's diet, and catching them is something of a caracal specialty. One of the fastest of all cats, the caracal can easily outrun a small gazelle. A nimble climber and jumper, it goes after nesting and roosting birds in the treetops and has been known to attack the martial eagle, one of the largest birds of prey. On the ground, surprising a flock of feeding pigeons, a caracal will characteristically pounce into their midst and begin a sort of frenzied dance, swiping right and left with its incredibly fast forepaws, leaping as high as six feet in the air to bat down fluttering birds. Before the surviving pigeons have made their escape, a caracal might fell as many as eight or ten birds.

Just how tame the hunting caracals of India actually become is a matter of speculation. Because they are so attractive-looking, humans have made many efforts, without much success, to domesticate them. The caracal is braver than other Small Cats and is reputedly the only one that will attack humans when it is disturbed at a kill. Armand Denis, the African wildlife authority, had a pet caracal that was tame enough most of the time but was subject to unpredictable "fits of wildness." Whenever it had such seizures, Denis reports, the cat would be immediately restored to purring amiability if it was presented with a saucer of milk.

Caracals are found in arid, hilly regions of Africa from the Mediterranean Sea to the Cape of Good Hope, as well as all over the Middle East and southern and central India. Once abundant over their range, they were hunted almost to extinction for their luxuriant fur until game laws were enacted to save them. The black, curly fur called Karakul does not, incidentally, come from a cat but from the newborn lambs of Karakul sheep. Caracals make their homes and bear their young in a hollow tree, under a rocky ledge, or in the preempted dens of aardvarks or porcupines.

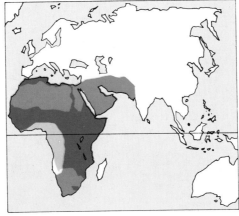

Servals (blue) range over central and northern Africa; caracals (red) inhabit Africa and Asia

A Talented Acrobat

The dainty, acrobatic serval is a small cat whose tawny coat is decorated with different-sized black spots and whose ears, neck, shoulders, and tail are marked with stripes. A distinctive feature is the serval's sharply pointed, uncat-like muzzle. The chance to watch a stalking serval is like happening on a private exhibition by a highly skilled gymnast. With back arched and paws curved inward, the serval executes astonishing high jumps that are controlled and precise. While it is not a strong animal, its unusual athletic skills enable it to catch the small animals it preys on.

The serval often lives near streams and preys on the small game that inhabits the thick bushes along the water's edge. Above, a hare has foolishly left its burrow in the deep grasses for the shorter, less protective turf within paw's reach of a partly tamed serval. Seconds later the hare is caught, quickly killed by a bite on the neck, and carried off to be eaten (right). Because of its nocturnal habits humans seldom get a glimpse of this elusive, leaping sleight-of-cat.

"Fast Hands" of a Caracal

The captive female caracal shown here provides a rarely photographed demonstration of its skill at trapping birds in midair. The incident itself passed as quickly as an accelerated reel of film. Several doves had landed within range of the caracal's exceptional hearing. With characteristic stealth the cat jumped in among them, causing panic as the doves attempted to escape. But the caracal's strong hind legs and swift front paws enable it to bat one from the air with ease (left). Caracals have been observed capturing as many as ten birds in this manner. The catch was immediately devoured in a most uncatlike way (below, right). Though small, the caracal is reputedly vicious, and it discourages close association with a display of its ferocity (below, left).

Ocelots and Other Small Cats

A native of the southwestern United States and Latin America, the ocelot (opposite) is a small cat of remarkable beauty. Also called the painted leopard and *tigrillo*, it has a gray-white fur dappled with black designs (some with reddish-brown centers) that are arranged in stripes or bands of rosettes along the body. The little cat has been favored for centuries as a somewhat exotic house pet, although some owners have learned to their pain and sorrow that it never completely abandons its wild nature. Cherished as much by hunters and trappers as by cat lovers, the ocelot has been hunted and trapped to the brink of extinction for its decorative fur and is now high on the list of endangered species.

Ocelots most often live in forests and tropical jungles but are also found in arid scrubland. Excellent climbers, they are able to hunt and take refuge in trees. Sometimes a pair of ocelots will live together, hunting as a team at night and calling back and forth to each other to maintain contact. Adult ocelots are three and one-half feet long, including their tails, and weigh from 30 to 35 pounds. In the tropics, there appears to be no seasonal breeding period, and mating may occur at any time of the year. In colder climates ocelots breed in the spring. The average litter is from two to four kittens.

There are dozens of other species of Small Cats that inhabit the remaining wildernesses of the Old and New Worlds. They vary widely in appearance but share several characteristics that distinguish them from the two other major cat species, Big Cats and Cheetahs. Size has nothing to do with the classification; the puma, a "small" cat, is as large as a leopard, a "big" cat. The primary differences are the Small Cat's inability to roar like a Big Cat and the way their eyes dilate. Small Cats' pupils narrow to a slit in bright light; Big Cats' contract as shrinking spheres, like human eyes.

The margay is almost a miniature reproduction of the ocelot—usually no larger than an ordinary house cat. Like the ocelot, the margay is hunted for its beautiful coat, which places it in grave danger of extinction. In the wild, margays are agile aerialists, scampering around on trees and vines as nimbly as monkeys or squirrels. They frequently jump from great heights—for no apparent reason and with no apparent ill effects. They are secretive creatures, living in the dense jungles from Mexico to Brazil, and not much is known about their life in the wild.

Jaguarundis are equally at home in water, brush, or jungle. They have flat, otterlike heads and are the scourge of rodent populations. Before the time of the Spanish conquistadors, Indians kept tamed jaguarundis as rat-killers, and they are still highly esteemed in Latin America as the exterminators of the rats that menace the rice harvests and carry epidemic diseases.

Pampas cats, with large reddish streaks on their silver coats, range the grasslands of Argentina and Uruguay, the Mato Grosso, and Andean South America. Geoffroy's cat lives in the lower reaches—up to 5,000 feet—of the Andes from Bolivia southward to Patagonia and wisely avoids man and his settlements. The black-footed cat once ranged over most of southern Africa but has retreated before advancing civilization to the point where it is now seen only rarely and in desert regions. The black-foot is the smallest of all felines, even smaller than the ordinary house cat. Adults measure no more than 14 inches, including a six-inch tail. A shy little cat, it comes out only at night, and its distinctive spotted markings are a scientific puzzle, for they serve no purpose as camouflage. Black-footed cats have been known to mate with domestic cats. Golden cats are divided into two species. One, the African golden cat, inhabits the rain forests of western Africa; another, Temminck's golden cat, lives in the jungles of Southeast Asia. They come in different sizes and a variety of colors, none of them precisely golden. The European wildcat is a size larger than a house cat and marked like a domestic tabby. As the Continent has become crowded with men and their cities, the European wildcat has retreated to the forests and mountains and hunts only at night. The long-haired Pallas' cat of central Asia is believed to be the ancestor of the domestic Persian cat.

What all these smaller and lesser-known cats have in common with one another and with the titans of the tribe, such as the lion, the tiger, and the leopard, is an extraordinary grace of form, coloration, and movement. As Leonardo da Vinci, who knew as much about beauty as any man who ever lived, noted centuries ago: "The smallest of the felines is a masterpiece."

Ocelots (red) are rare in the United States, more common in Central and South America.

The Smallest Members of the Family

By far the most numerous, most diversified members of the feline family trinity are in the Small Cat branch. There are just four designated Big Cats, one type of Cheetah in a category of its own, and two transitional species with characteristics of both the Small and the Big Cats. Small Cats number no fewer than 30 different species, ranging from the leopard-sized puma to the tiny African black-footed cat. They vary not just in size but in appearance as well. The fuzzy, compact Pallas' cat seems to be a completely different kind of animal from the slim, long-legged, blue-eyed domestic Siamese. And yet they are not only unmistakably cats; they are cousins. The cats shown on these and the following pages are all different, all beautiful, and all certifiably Small Cats. It was a Small Cat, the ancestor of today's house cat, that was first venerated as a god by the ancient Egyptians. And it is a Small Cat that has traveled with modern man, if not as a god, at least as a dignified companion, to every corner of the earth.

Unlike other little cats, whose fur may be decorated with spots, rings, rosettes, or stripes, the jaguarundi has a plain coat that may range from a reddish brown to a charcoal gray that sometimes approaches black. This wildcat is slightly larger than the common domestic cat, having a 20-inch-long body and a king-sized 16-inch tail. In Latin America the jaguarundi's legendary chicken-raiding exploits have earned the elusive predator (above) a reputation for supernatural hunting powers.

The languid, exotically marked Marbled cat (above), a rare
Oriental beauty, haunts the forests and jungles of Southeast
Asia from the Himalayas to Borneo. Virtually every part of
its body is splashed, like a Jackson Pollock canvas, with
asymmetrical spots and specks. Another uncommonly
beautiful tree-dweller is the margay of Central and South
America (opposite, below), which looks so much like a
miniaturized version of the ocelot that their pelts are often
confused. An incomparable aerialist, it leaves the trees only
to hunt and will dangle nonchalantly by one hind foot from
the highest branches.

121

The leopard cat (above) is an aristocrat that only vaguely resembles its much larger namesake. Its "stripes" are actually elongated spots. It has a range across eastern and central Asia.

A Clowder of

The cats shown on these pages are representative of the great variety and remarkable adaptability of the Small Cats of Europe, Africa, and Asia. They inhabit the frosty highlands of Scotland, the steaming rain forests of Africa, the Himalayan foothills of India, and the torrid jungles of Indonesia. The Scottish wildcat at left is an isolated subspecies of the European wildcat that developed its thick fur during the Ice Age, when it retreated to the forests. It still retains the warm-weather instincts of its brethren on the more temperate Continent, however, and comes out to hunt in winter only during the warmest part of the day. At the easternmost extremity of the Old World cats' range, the

122

The golden cat comes in two species, both forest-dwellers: Temminck's golden cat (above) ranges from eastern India and China throughout Southeast Asia; the African golden cat is native to the rain forests of West Africa.

Old World Cats

Temminck's golden cat, above, adapted to its environment in some curious ways. Even though they are excellent climbers, Temminck's cats will not bother to pursue any animal that climbs up a tree above eye level, apparently because the hunting is better on the forest floor. The African black-footed cat, right, has learned to survive on the edges of the Sahara by restricting its activity to the cooler hours of night. Wherever they may be, these versatile little cats have made some remarkable changes in their habits to conform with their sometimes changing environment and have undergone evolutionary changes that enable them to survive where less adaptable animals have become extinct.

123

The cat above seems the picture of a cuddly, curious domestic house pet that would be quite at home curled up before a roaring fire. Actually it is the untamed, aptly named European wildcat.

And this angry creature, with its hair bristling and every muscle and nerve fiber tensed to pounce on its quarry, while related to all the other wildcats, is none other than the amiable Persian. The domestic house cat has adapted to man and civilization far more successfully than any of its wild cousins.

At home in every climate and continent, domestic cats number more than 35 million in the U.S. alone.

Credits

All photographs in this book, including the one on the cover, are by John Dominis, except those listed below.

1—Nancy Crampton. 5—Thase Daniel. 6—(top, center) Dmitri Kessel, T-L P.A., (lower left) Stan Wayman, T-L P.A. 16—Dmitri Kessel, T-L P.A. 17—Dmitri Kessel, T-L P.A. 18—(top) Frank W. Lane. 19—Bruce Coleman from Bruce Coleman, Inc. 22—(top) Nigel A. Dundas from Bruce Coleman, Inc., (bottom) Clem Haagner. 23—Norman Myers from Bruce Coleman, Inc. 25—Jean-Erick Pasquier from Rapho/Photo Researchers, Inc. 26-27—(top) David Goodnow. 34—Peter Davey from Frank W. Lane. 45—Co Rentmeester, T-L P.A. 46-47—Stan Wayman, T-L P.A. 48—Tom McHugh from Photo Researchers, Inc. 49—Plage from Bruce Coleman, Inc. 50—Stan Wayman, T-L P.A. 51—Stan Wayman, T-L P.A. 52—Co Rentmeester, T-L P.A. 54—Richard Waller from Ardea Photographics. 55—Marc and Evelyne Bernheim from Woodfin Camp and Associates. 74—(top) Nina Leen, T-L P.A. 75—George B. Schaller from Bruce Coleman, Inc. 79—Dmitri Kessel, T-L P.A. 80—Loren McIntyre from Woodfin Camp and Associates. 81—Dmitri Kessel, T-L P.A. 83—Ralph Crane, T-L P.A. 84—T. W. Hall from Bruce Coleman, Inc. 86—Jen and Des Bartlett from Bruce Coleman, Inc. 87—T. W. Hall from Bruce Coleman, Inc. 88—Dmitri Kessel, T-L P.A. 100—Bruce Coleman from Bruce Coleman, Inc. 101—Peter Davey from Frank W. Lane 103—Ted Gorsline from Bruce Coleman, Inc. 104—Tom McHugh/Wildlife Unlimited from Photo Researchers, Inc. 105—Juan Fernandez from Bruce Coleman, Inc. 106—Carl Iwasaki, T-L P.A. 107—Tom McHugh/Wildlife Unlimited from Photo Researchers, Inc. 108—Gary N. Hill 109—Ernest Wilkinson 110-111—Stouffer Productions Ltd. from Bruce Coleman, Inc. 119—Dmitri Kessel, T-L P.A. 120-121—Diane and Rick Sullivan from Bruce Coleman, Inc. 122—(top) Bruce Coleman, Inc., (bottom) Jane Burton from Bruce Coleman, Inc. 123—(top) Diane and Rick Sullivan from Bruce Coleman, Inc., (bottom) Nina Leen, T-L P.A. 124—Hans Reinhard from Bruce Coleman, Inc. 125—Stephen Green-Armitage from Photo Researchers, Inc.

Photographs on endpapers are used courtesy of Time-Life Picture Agency and Russ Kinne and Stephen Dalton of Photo Researchers, Inc.

Film sequences and individual frames are from "Leopard!," "The Social Cat," and "African Waterhole," programs in the Time-Life Television series *Wild, Wild World of Animals*.

MAPS on pages 14, 44, 56, 78, 82, 92, 102, 112 and 118 are by Demi Hitz.

DIAGRAMS on pages 9, 12, and 13 are by Eve Cellini. Diagrams on pages 10, 98 and 99 are by Arthur Singer.

ILLUSTRATIONS on pages 28–31, 62–67, 76–77 and 88–91 are by Douglas Gorsline. Drawings on pages 76–77 are adapted from the original photographs of Carl Akeley taken on location in Africa, used by permission of the American Museum of Natural History. Illustration on page 73 is by Andre Durenceau.

Bibliography

Adamson, Joy, *Born Free: A Lioness of Two Worlds*. Pantheon, 1960.

———*Elsa*. Pantheon, 1963.

Akeley, Carl, and Akeley, Mary L. Jobe, *Lions, Gorillas and Their Neighbors*. Stanley Paul, 1931.

Allen, Thomas B., editor, *The Marvels of Animal Behavior*. National Geographic Society, 1972.

Boorer, Michael, *Wild Cats*. Bantam Books, 1971.

Boulenger, E. G., *Wild Life the World Over*. William H. Wise & Co., Inc., 1947

Caras, Roger A., *North American Mammals*. Meredith Press, 1967.

Corbett, Jim, *Man-Eaters of India*. Oxford University Press, 1957.

Curry-Lindahl, Kai, and Harroy, Jean-Paul, *National Parks of the World*, Volumes 1 and 2, A Golden Field Guide. Golden Press, 1972.

Denis, Armand, *Cats of the World*. Houghton Mifflin, 1964.

Dinesen, Isak, *Out of Africa*. Random House, 1970.

Dominis, John, and Edey, Maitland, *The Cats of Africa*. Time-Life Books, 1968.

Eaton, Randall, *The Cheetah*. Van Nostrand Reinhold Company, 1974.

Eaton, Randall, editor, *The World's Cats*, Volumes 1 and 2. World Widelife Safari, Oregon, 1975.

The Editors of Time-Life Books, *Vanishing Species*. Time-Life Books, 1974.

Fichter, George S., *Cats*. Golden Press, 1973.

Grzimek, Bernard, *Grzimek's Animal Life Encyclopedia*, 12 Mammals III. Van Nostrand Reinhold Company, 1975.

Guggisberg, C.A.W., *Simba*. Chilton Books, 1963.

———*Wild Cats*. Taplinger, 1975.

Haas, Emmy, *Pride's Progress: The Story of a Family of Lions*. Harper & Row, 1967.

Leopold, A. Starker, *Wildlife of Mexico: The Game Birds and Mammals*. University of California Press, 1959.

Muldoon, Guy, *Leopards in the Night*. Appleton-Century-Crofts, 1954.

Perry, Richard, *The World of the Jaguar*. Taplinger, 1970.

———*The World of the Tiger*. Atheneum, 1964.

Roosevelt, Theodore, *African Game Trails*. Charles Scribner's Sons, 1910.

Rudnai, Judith, *The Social Life of the Lion*. Washington Square East, Publishers, 1973.

Schaller, George B., *Deer and the Tiger: A Study of Wildlife in India*. University of Chicago Press, 1967.

———*Golden Shadows, Flying Hooves*. Alfred A. Knopf, Inc., 1973.

———*Serengeti: A Kingdom of Predators*. Alfred A. Knopf, Inc., 1972.

———*The Serengeti Lion: A Study in Predator-Prey Relations*. University of Chicago Press, 1972.

Selous, Frederick C., *African Nature Notes and Reminiscences*. The Macmillan Company, 1908.

Turnbull-Kemp, Peter, *The Leopard*. Bailey Brothers and Swinfen, 1967.

Van Wormer, Joe, *World of the Bobcat*. Lippincott, 1964.

Varaday, Desmond, *Gara Yaka, the Story of a Cheetah*. Ballantine, 1974.

Young, Stanley P., *The Bobcat of North America*. The Stackpole Co., Harrisburg, Pennsylvania, and The Wildlife Management Institute, Washington, D.C., 1958.

Young, Stanley P., and Goldman, Edward A., *Puma: Mysterious American Cat*. Dover, 1946.

Index

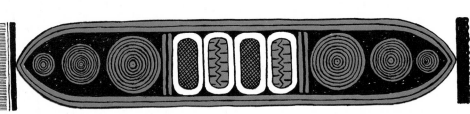
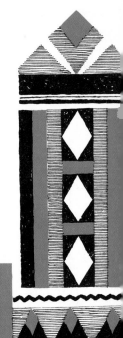